LET THE WORDS
SELECTED POEMS

YONA WALLACH

LET THE WORDS
SELECTED POEMS

YONA WALLACH

Translated by Linda Stern Zisquit

THE SHEEP MEADOW PRESS
RIVERDALE-ON-HUDSON, NY

All inquiries and permission requests should be addressed to:
The Sheep Meadow Press
P.O. Box 1345
Riverdale-on-Hudson, NY 10471

Designed and typeset by The Sheep Meadow Press.
Distributed by The University Press of New England.

Printed on acid-free paper in the United States. This book meets the guidelines for permanence and durability of the Committee on Production Guidelines for Book Longevity of the Council on Library Resources.

Library of Congress Cataloging-in-Publication Data

Wallach, Yona.
Let the words : selected poems of Yona Wallach / translated by Linda Stern Zisquit.
    p. cm.
Includes bibliographical references.
ISBN 1-931357-34-X (alk. paper)
I. Zisquit, Linda. II. Title.

PJ5054.W26L47 2006
892.4'16--dc22

2005036254

ACKNOWLEDGMENTS

Some of these translations have appeared in *The American Poetry Review, Ariel, The Jerusalem Post, The Jerusalem Review, The Harvard Review, Maggid, Mediterraneans, Modern Poetry in Translation, Pequod, Shirim,* and *Tikkun.*

"On Yona Wallach" by Aharon Shabtai was previously published in *Haderim.*

I am grateful to the National Endowment for the Arts for a Translation Grant I received in 1996 to help finish *Wild Light: Selected Poems of Yona Wallach.*

CONTENTS

from TWO GARDENS (1969)

from COLLECTED POEMS (1976)

from WILD LIGHT (1983)

from FORMS (1985)

from APPEARANCE (1985)

from SELECTED POEMS (1992)
(posthumous poems)

ON YONA WALLACH
by Aharon Shabtai

ONE EVENING, when I was in Tel Aviv, someone knocked on the door, brought her in, and left. With little or nothing by way of introductions or pleasantries a friendship formed, and over the course of a month we met often, until I came to my senses and went back to my regular routine and my studies in Jerusalem. I was older and, in retrospect, it seems that for a little while at least I played the role of a father figure. Yona herself was always creating a father and destroying a father at one and the same time. She would wander around in her beatniky get-up and way, wasting time, astonishing and horrifying the people who were sitting at the Frak Café. This was how she explained herself to herself, how she was able to disintegrate and reconstruct or regenerate herself. This was her logos. My story, on the other hand, was about creating parents for myself through the sphere of growth (work, education). The parents she reconstructed were demons of a kind—the pursuing-pursued non-parents of a schizoid-paranoid perspective. The parents I created for myself were connected to the ethos and poetics of experience. I'd written a poem (largely drawn from a dream) about a vegetable garden; I wrote it with great excitement and felt that I had suddenly located for myself the mode of parents. The "I" was placed between parentheses, as though it hadn't yet been born, but a mode was created that would make its birth possible. The contact with tools, or machines (a tractor, for instance), showed me that a certain gravity or weight exists, that it is possible to locate structure, rules, and forces—to internalize all this, in other words, to reconstruct a cultural and psychological syntax. The twenty-year-old Yona Wallach, however, was a mystic from the start. She sought out "life's revelation," though this sort of knowledge—"which no man could see and live"—meant death, meant becoming an I that was not-I; revealing life, in other words, meant leaving life behind—carrying out on oneself a sparagasmos (a Dionysian act of dismemberment), and so, according to the modal logic of the experience, depression and anxiety were transformed into a mania:

> Yes. I take that upon myself. There was Jesus and after him there had to be Yona. God wanted to be revealed again on the stage of history, and one can't continue without Him. Life is pointless without God. Maybe He wasn't particularly thrilled that I found him. Maybe this is one of those cosmic catastrophes, something that neither He nor I brought on, and there are other gods beyond God. This is the God of the middle, but there is another god of nature, who creates us and is the true god, the enormous and powerful god, and we're in his hands, we're his tools. And it may just be that my fate was to reveal him. Take the poem "Black Hand"—how could I have written a poem like that? I wrote it without thinking, it was totally unconscious. I was simply a medium. I'm a parapsychologist, I have senses. I'm a mystic. I take hold of the forces of the world.

The knowledge evident here is clearly a "gnosis." Yona's behavior could be described along the lines both of Melanie Klein's theories and those of the Kabbala: she splits, she's split, she gives birth to herself and in the process empties herself and is annihilated as a microcosm and a macrocosm. She descends among the husks in order to raise up the sparks, or shatters the husks with the force of the sparks within her. She doesn't sit home, as she puts it, and cultivate her soul; she runs around with perverts and crooks—she distinguishes between them (between their embryonic self) and their husks (the labels imposed on them from outside). Each one of them she sees "with his very own eyes."

The concept of self is critical in this context, and without it one simply cannot understand Yona Wallach. On the one hand Yona is an example of a selfless person; her story, like Artaud's, is that the self is stolen away with birth. She is overly split, invaded by foreign I's, and so in fact doesn't exist (emotionally) in the here and now.

Basic aspects of life are familiar to her only in a cerebral manner: she creates words, but not life, in the sense that life is created when one knows how to make use of love—something Yona doesn't know. In gnosis, and in mysticism as well, there is a degree of lifelessness—on the one hand the music of the spheres, on the other a kind of arid compulsion, detachment, and esotericism. All these are factors I felt coming through in her poems. Nevertheless, her major contribution was that she introduced to Hebrew literature the language of the self. She shattered the scarecrow of the I (as a self-contained object whose contents and qualities precede language), and she began to speak in an absolute manner about the world, where "making the object" always meant "making the self." There is a fixed, established I, but in her view there is another I, an I who, in poetry, has all sorts of opportunities to change. These things she says as a "parapsychologist" and a born mystic: "I was born this way, my grandfather was a mystic in Russia. To this day people make pilgrimages to his grave, to pray for fertility."

I'm thinking now about that brief encounter between us. My temperament was rabbinic from the start, and the quarrel between the rabbis and the mystics is an old one; it was already in evidence when the editing of the Bible took place and the apocalyptic and gnostic books were rejected, along with Jesus. My state of mind was Pharisaic: one first of all had to carry out life's tasks and the daily ritual and liturgical cycles in order for knowledge to accrue through the particular rhythms of experience (rejection, delay, breakthrough, resistance, compromise, practice). The emphasis here is on repetition and practice as a basis for variation and change. This is a problem the Talmudic sages are well aware of when they discuss prayer, and specifically the fact that, because it is a daily practice, it requires a kind of estrangement. And thus one arrives at the notion of rightness or purity of intention, *kavannah*. All shortcuts, therefore, are tantamount to a kind of amateurism; from the rabbinic point of view, there are no shortcuts to gnosis. The day the Temple was destroyed, revelation and prophecy ceased to exist. On the other hand, the Torah as the basis of the kabbalistic Zohar, as a model for the act of creation, of genesis, contains within it all the mystic (revelatory) elements of the self. And in this sense I feel a profound affinity with Yona Wallach. In her poems and in interviews she speaks of faith. This is why, she notes, she broke off relations with her closest friends: "The blow-up was caused by my religious beliefs. They simply couldn't understand that. So I cut myself off from them."

This, as I see it, is the crossroads where Hebrew literature stands today. For me as well, religion (in the non-institutional sense) is our language—Judaism is internalized in us as a language of the self and of fate, to distinguish it from the Platonic language that deals with concepts and ideas about "what exists." The self is the great mystery of the name (how the name as a text is evident within, creating us, and how it is evident without, as exterior, in the language of facts). The Jews (in contrast to the Platonists) believe in the name, decode the name, and all the attributes and contents in this context, such as "the chosen," "the holy," are in fact connected to spiritual birth and creation. Plato and his descendants emphasized the importance of aletheia (truth) in contrast to doxa (opinion, faith, the imaginary); therefore the poets were banished, along with the sophists and the mystics, and rationalism reigned. Today the circle has come round and we've returned to the pre-Socratics—to sages like Gorgias, who insisted on the divinity of language (myth, logos) and showed how people locate facts and create concepts in accordance with their faith and persuasion. The world is a multiplication of doxa, and if we don't understand what faith is, we lack the concepts with which we might speak either of the self or of the real (of realities). Human beings declare that they do not believe in God, but the self (if one listens carefully enough) is, in its way, always talking about God, about angels and demons. Sometimes it seems that this is the only conversation it's possible to hear. And in this sense Yona Wallach's poetry is primal.

But first things first. In 1965, after all, I didn't know what to do with the language of the self. I was under the influence of the epic and its ethos, that of Hesiod in particular. During my first year of university studies I happened onto a lecture by Paolo Vivente on archaic poetry.

It was winter; the windows of the first-floor classroom rattled loudly in the wind and the rain, and he read, in English, and powerfully, from Hesiod's *Works and Days*, a poem that astonished me and opened up before me a world of gods, forces, work, elements, and time. For Hesiod the world isn't a given. Wisdom, mythically, is power, like shrewdness, but these capacities aren't mutually exclusive; they become manifest in a continuity that involves chaos, chance, necessity, and fate. The poem teaches the farmer what to do at all times of the year in order to exist and survive in the iron age, in a world that received fire and craft from Prometheus, and sorrow, sickness, Eros, and cunning from Pandora. It teaches one, for instance, how to put on a hat in winter so as not to catch a cold and die. The poem simply amazed me; suddenly I was hearing a music that wasn't decadent. This encounter was formative for my relation to the worn-out material that constituted the lyric I.

Around that time, Yona gave me some pages from a notebook with her "Island Poems #1;" this was in Tel Aviv. Later on I spent a weekend with her in her hometown of Kiryat Ono. That Saturday afternoon we sat on the porch, and I spoke with reservation about the hybrid quality of the poems she'd given me. I was looking for a direct, clear rhetoric without eccentricity, and so I didn't like her early poems—about Jonathan, Cecilia, Sebastian, Antonia, and so on. It all seemed somehow capricious to me, and deep down I felt they gave off a sense of illness and satisfaction with illness. I think that the blindness I displayed at the time had its place, that it was vital in fact, and emerged from a correct reading of her mode. And Yona too became conscious in her poems and in interviews of the masochism that had taken root in our literature and, as a means of reflecting on life, backed it into a dead end:

> That's the most serious thing about poetry, that it likes to be miserable, and not actually say things, not solve problems, not be wise. It likes to teach people to be miserable, and to think melancholy thoughts and build the future in abjection and then be ill.
>
> (*Hadarim* 4, interview)

The compelling quality about misery is that it is an inviolable narcissistic stance. But misery and illness have distinct contents of various sorts. I know now from my own experience that sometimes we get sick when we need to learn something about ourselves. The illness reconstructs a situation of imaginary health. For the self has rhythms of progress within retreat, of health within sickness; one needs not-to-know in order to know, to destroy in order to build. If it weren't for chance, fate, illness, repression, we'd be walking computers. Donald Winnicott (in the two green volumes of his articles from Hogarth Press) talks about the relation between the true self and the false self. The true self is "the bad child" that expresses itself, that seeks connection and therefore also destroys (because the true lover is the one that can't be destroyed). But paradoxically there is also a need for the false self—that "good child" within us, so that it can defend the true self from extreme exposure, which would be tantamount to "rape of the self." Yona, it turns out, was speaking in a code that I couldn't understand at the time. By splitting into characters, and shifting from gender to gender, she was telling her first story, her "theogony"—which was born to give birth to her progenitors. The story of the first minute of life is that the infant finds a parent (actually); or vice versa, the roles are reversed and the parent finds in the infant a parent who will fulfill him or her and offer emotional nourishment. The infant then becomes the parent. From there on everything is demonic and under tremendous pressure, for things can no longer be located in their proper place. The parent is God, but this God is actually Yona, and promptly turns into Satan, a haunting figure and a threat to existence; for it murdered the infant and in doing so stole (through Yona) Yona's identity. Yona is the baby that hasn't yet been born—that exists only in thought, in the mind of another, who in turn is only a thought in her head. Yona operates in this way often in her work. Her job is to give birth to herself, but that birth involves necessity, according to the rhythm I've described—the rhythms of the illness. When the baby is the parent, everything is inverted and each object becomes its opposite: "Good turns into evil, the violence of pain become pleasant, and vice versa of course/ and sound turns into matter and matter in turn to anti-matter and knowledge to anti-knowledge/ and the real becomes what's imagined, and vice versa, and you are anti-you," and so, "emotion like an atom's nucleus post-explosion gives off maximum radioactivity/ in the unorganized dispersal of fall-out" ("Hierarchy").

We're isolating a central concept here—the illness—and trying to understand its content as experience and pioneer knowledge, total knowledge, because that was the thing that in February 1965 impressed me so forcefully about Yona's personality, apart from her poems: the transition from writing in the limited sense of the term to total writing—writing in action, in objects, in sex, in the body and in the body-soul complex. In meeting her, then, each act betrayed more than it would have ordinarily. Critical margins were widened, all focus was split. I remember that she made a salad and served it up at the table on the porch. In retrospect (even if I don't remember what I was thinking at the time) I see the salad "written out"—as a hieroglyph. The salad is a confession of the I, and accordingly, since the I is imagined, the salad becomes its embodiment.

That said, I'm sitting on the porch twenty years ago in Kiryat Ono, looking at the salad as a hieroglyph which is a minuscule part of the larger hieroglyph of the garden—an ordinary garden in that part of the country, the house at its center, and at its edge a structure of some sort, a kind of closed-in hut with a makeshift roof that once served, I imagine, as a chicken coop. That's Yona's dove-cote: Yona (*yona* in Hebrew means dove) who is an object, a thing, and therefore a bird (flight is the fluttering of possibilities; in Plato, as well, in *Theaetetus*, things are doves, *yonim*, in a cage). And, as everyone knows, since a dove is a bird whose nature is quite different from its image, so the things-birds are sometimes tame and sometimes shriek within the "I" like birds of prey or scavengers. This is the garden of childhood, and it's described as a framework for the primal event in a number of her poems. The garden is a framework for spiritual embodiment; the various animals, like the doe, are according to Yona "states of consciousness," "not identification." The problem, after all, is that there is no one with whom to identify, and so out of necessity the doe becomes the monster:

But in each beast there's a monster
just as in each bird there is something weird
just as a monster exists in each person

The monstrous garden: this is the body-soul complex. For Yona, "we make the face," and what there is (or isn't) in the soul extends across the body, and the spiritual-bodily garden is therefore the topography of illness; this is the "evil garden" of the poem "Layers," in which there exists "the evil gardener" and layers and layers of choice farm-soil that is made into "dead dirt," while "in an evil layer much deeper within" there lies a kind of "blackening heart," "a criminal seed," which is traumatic. This is the "biographical disaster" that spills across the other layers as a bitter poison, a cancerous tissue, and the disaster by necessity returns as a "model" of the fact that the future is always the past.

The garden includes what the self is capable of writing and telling about itself, and therefore we have here a drama: a struggle with fate within a passage through fate. Fate is established, but not along the lines of the Platonic myth of choice (at the end of *The Republic*), where one chooses a well-defined kind of life for the future in the form of an idea that has content, content which can be located through the analysis of concepts. The contents of fate require deciphering within character—thus Heraclitus states that character (*ethos*) is fate (*daimon*). This is precisely where one finds Yona Wallach's radicality, and that radicality astonished me even then, in 1965, when she had herself hospitalized. Rimbaud said that "true life is elsewhere," that "I is someone else," that the poet needs to be the possessor of unique knowledge—"a seer." In his famous letter he writes that, for this reason, in order to arrive at the unknown, the senses must be fundamentally deranged and one has to be (among other things) "the great patient." But the positivism of the period defeated him. He sought a manner in which he could be authentic, and was able to discern all possible embodiments of life, narcissistic models, masks of the bourgeois theater, even of the "adventurer," the "saint," the "outlaw," or "bohemian." All of these seemed to him finally like puppets (to take up the title of one of Yona's poems). So that in the end he chose raw experience: "I! I who have called myself a sorcerer and angel, am free of all morality, and return to the earth which I will explore, to embrace crude reality! A farmer!"

Rimbaud despaired of ever getting beyond consciousness—beyond its creative derangement, illness—to a cosmic language, and he began dreaming of raising a son who would be an engineer. But in retrospect, his exile in Harar, his wound in the jungle, the putrefaction of his leg and his dying in the hospital in Marseilles were all an extension of the writing. Indeed Artaud wrote consciously from within his illness (mental illness). This is the subject of his correspondence (beginning in 1923) with the editor of *La nouvelle revue française*, Jacques Rivère. Artaud takes great pains to emphasize that, in contrast to the psychological automatism of the surrealists, his own writing is based on a flaw in the soul as the ground of primary writing. This is writing from within the womb, before God came along and created classification—generalizing intelligence, which rendered the entire world demonic and poisonous. God stole the body from Artaud, and Artaud—who saved himself (from the illness of health, from the poison of life)—describes himself as someone who was reborn "as a body without organs" (in other words, without the internalization of foreign I's). And so, as an absolute orphan, having negated what today we'd call "sexism," he is capable of declaring: "I, Antonin Artaud, am my son, my father, my mother, and my self." These, then, are the contents of "the theater of cruelty"—the murder of God the father, the deliverance of the body from all text, which is to say, from the narcissistic invasion of imagism and foreign consciousness and the splitting of eroticization.

The language here is that of Yona Wallach; and Artaud, too, spoke in terms of cults and mystics. One might compare Yona's poems from *Forms* to series such as "Artaud the Momo" or "To Annihilate the Sentence of God." Clearly in a world where schizoid reality is established as the norm, illness becomes the key to understanding the language of fate—the daimon which is *ethos*. This is the tone of the letters I received from Talbieh, where Yona was hospitalized. She was preparing herself to be a *voyant* and arranging for herself a kind mental maternity ward: comparing drugs, medicines, and wines, and talking about birth—each drug was a different birth and a different kind of nourishment or way of nursing. From there on she has, as she put it, "a double life." At the hospital, as though in recognition of her special status, she received a large room with wonderful acoustics, and from its window one could see the wall of the Old City ("which, for certain people here, has turned into a wall that has to be gone over"). At the same time she lived in the city. I helped her rent a room not far from my own, on the third floor of the Notre Dame Monastery.

The most important thing that happened to Hebrew poetry in 1965, then, was the discovery of the language of the self, the language of a double life. One no longer said "either this or that," and "that equals that," but "this and that," and "that's different from that." This is the wisdom that Yona inherited from "her fathers the magical hunters." She speaks about a mystical light, which she distinguishes from the light of day; this mystical "wild light," which bestows "understanding of the doubleness within her," is a light that takes darkness into account (the dimension in which things are other than themselves and nameless), and only in this synthetic light ("artificial daylight") can one grasp things as general and particular, as nameless and possessors of name and meaning.

The illness is therefore that necessary night, without which it is impossible to arrive at "the hidden inner light." This is the way down which is the way up; this is Yona's way. The word "fascist" inevitably gives rise to repulsive associations, but I say—if one wants to exist in the spiritual sense, not only as a false self, "a good child"— one has to discover the fascist within oneself and use it as a kind of resource. This is our one true natural resource, and this is the gist of Yona's mysticism—that these terrible internalizations (and a child always has to internalize what there is, to play the role he's forced to play), all the poison of the "evil garden," that Hades, is our store of gold, if, of course, beyond our knowledge of superficial moralism, we learn how to grant ourselves what our parents didn't know how to offer us—reception, understanding, attention. In *The Eumenides* of Aeschylus there appear the Erinyes: their eyes drip blood; snakes crawl through their hair. They are the emissaries of Clytemnestra, the monstrous mother, who take existence (from her family and her self). Athena points at them and says, roughly: "Don't pay attention to that awful sight, this is the hidden treasure that you have as human beings and Athenians." Unlike the idea, which is the embodiment of the law of contradiction, fate is always double. Yona's illness tells of the night without name, in which there is no emotional existence. This idea runs through *Forms* like a scarlet thread.

When a person turns into a "good child," embodying another, he turns into a puppet and at the same time becomes a monster. Therefore when the angels are internalized they are always monsters and demons. I too am shocked when I listen to arguments between people personifying angels. From Yona, as I've said, it's possible to learn why, when you personify an angel, you are actually a monster. She knows how to listen with the "inner ear" to the person within. The illness, then, is to go through birth once again as a not-I, to be united with the not-I, and to reconstruct, while learning the language of the self, the continuity of the I–not-I. This is a language that wasn't available to Rimbaud. In the end he drew back from being "someone beside himself," without understanding that this is part of being oneself: "To return to undivided consciousness/ not to fear consciousness split/ to be himself and not himself/ to speak about him as himself nothing/ to be non-existent in consciousness/ to be an object unto himself/ to be himself a subject/ while the function of strangeness/ is a single element set off by a name/ like this voice which speaks of him/ the stranger within him attended to/ becoming a voice in union" (*Forms*).

And this is something that few people understand—that it's impossible and even undesirable to rid oneself of trauma, to rid one's consciousness of the layer where the monster lies. One can only listen to it, and then, as Yona writes, "the knowledge [it offers] turns into a softer material." On the plane of the poisoned garden of the body-soul, the illness is the language of health; language is our oxygen, it creates health. On the plane of the garden, then, when the demonic elements are recognized, recognized and not rejected, but, on the contrary, accepted as they are (as imagination, as a creation and a vital part of oneself), an integration of the double is achieved, of the object with its opposite, which protects it. And so all becomes secure: a man in this way protects a woman, a bird its offspring, and the I itself finds a creative way of protecting itself "while all this is covered with letters and numbers," and the superfluous becomes the vital:

> like each thing that's inverted protected
> in its magical wondrous inversion protected
> by the sword that revolves every–which–way
> at the blocked entrance to Eden's Garden

So, in this manner, we can say that illness belongs to the forces of life. Life demands dismantling, not only construction. The force of the shocking illness requires the creation of new codes and syntax, requires the operation of puppets, hollow masks suddenly filled with blood and life, the recycling of all emotional waste. As in the poems of John Donne, the synthetic effort in Yona's work creates a meta-physical poetry. Its object is so profoundly heterogeneous (in the sense of the gaps, displacements, differences in quality) that, in the effort to contain and construct the whole, a new order is created, one that is more just, more enlightened. Yona manages to bring to-gether body and soul, consciousness, gender, and emotion, and from Hell creates an Eden. One must listen carefully: when day and night are conceived of as an unbroken unit (wherein night is understood as part of the day), we come to a situation in which all things have a name, but that name is the place, the very garden which is a spiri-tual/emotional place (when, spiritually, one knows how to put each thing in its place):

> to be busy for hours in place
> to lose track of place and time
> to begin again at the start

> meaning, the place
> to know that to start from the start
> is again to be in place

Faith plays a major role in this poetry, in the allegorization developed in the language of the self. Its subject is the name, place, God, the act of creation, the creation of the garden, of man (in the image of God), of the sexes. In this sense, *Forms*, the book in which her poetry achieves its greatest clarity and complexity, seems to me the Magna Carta of Hebrew poetry in our generation. That book, by virtue of its authority, teaches us how to free ourselves as writers and readers from our condition as exiles within our own land and our own culture. The book's principle message is that a person is what he thinks and knows about himself, that there is no content prior to language, to soul, to the metaphorical nature of things. In "Let Me Find You," she writes that "thoughts and visions are actual things."

And so we come round to the poetics of knowledge and vision. This is the tone of the entire book—that the poet knows, that he or she holds the key to the creative processes which constitute an ongoing Genesis. For there is, again, no pure object prior to language: the Torah is the model, and the world is first of all writing (Ibn Gabirol's poem comes to mind here: "Autumn wrote with its showers and ink..."). In this context it's important to mention as well the role of the imperative, which is so prominent in Yona's work. This imperative has a specific function, namely, it turns the illness into a kind of therapy, and the therapy, in turn, gives way to an entire and superior kind of pedagogy of emotion, of character, value, and intelligence. And so the manner of love is no longer to open up sentimental expanses, but, initially and primarily, to rehabilitate and educate the self:

> Let me see you truly
> and not through my own thoughts and feelings
> Let me see you through the good void
> of hand brain and soul

these after all are actual things
take me now as I am
it will be easy, then, to find you

Here, as throughout this work, one senses the condition and severity of a feverish, didactic, and metaphysical urgency, an urgency characteristic of a psychomania—a drama (like that of Dr. Faustus) wherein the struggle is for the immortality of the soul. This struggle serves as a mirror to everything that takes place in the body, in nature, and existence:

Don't let the living heart die within you and in me—
the subtle death of the moment is a dying emotion
the like of which for togetherness is
the sudden loss of the galaxy

—*translated by Peter Cole*

Editor's Note: This essay was written by Shabtai shortly before Yona Wallach's death in 1985. The publisher believes it will be of interest to readers of Wallach and Shabtai.

ON TRANSLATING YONA WALLACH

In 1982 I translated several of Yona Wallach's early poems in response to the request of a friend then editing an issue of Hebrew poetry for *The Literary Review.* I had reservations: my Hebrew was new, and Wallach's reputation—as a masterful poet who fragmented syntax with demonic power and broke laws of male and female conjugation—was intimidating. From the first, I felt myself pulled into a whirlwind, challenged by Wallach's brilliance, and charged by her contrariness. More than a need to enter the sensibility of an important poet, I felt an instinctive pull toward that mysterious space out of which Wallach speaks—where nothing is absolute and everything is in constant flux and the self remains unfixed. As though there were no choice, only an organic imperative requiring my energy to match hers, I have continued the project over these years.

The Selected Poems of Yona Wallach 1963-1985 was first published in Israel in 1992. Her other books include *Things* (1966), *Two Gardens* (1969), *Collected Poems* (1976), *Wild Light* (1983), *Forms* (1985) and *Appearance* (1985). Though Wallach died in 1985 at the age of 41, her work still exerts a major influence on poets writing in Hebrew today.

The history of modern Hebrew poetry is a series of formal rebellions waged by the leading poets responding not only to changes in the culture but also to a rapidly developing spoken tongue. The language that Yona Wallach was born into is almost unrecognizable from the Hebrew of a hundred years earlier. In 1897 Eliezer Ben Yehuda, responsible for compiling the first modern Hebrew dictionary in Jerusalem and credited with successfully launching the Hebrew speaking movement in Palestine, called on women to revive "this old, forgotten, dry and hard language—by permeating it with emotion, tenderness, suppleness and subtlety." Till the turn of the century Hebrew was primarily the language of the Book, confined to the study hall and synagogue; chanted, recited, it was the language of family observances and communal festivities, legal documents, and in some cases religious and secular poetry. Chaim Nachman Bialik, born in Russia and writing his most important work there, can be seen as a bridge between the 'Haskala' movement (1781-1871) in Europe—when Jews from Orthodox backgrounds labored to express secular ideas from the cultural Enlightenment in the 'holy tongue'—and the revival of Hebrew in Palestine. Writing in Odessa between 1890 and 1920, Bialik, "the poet of the national renaissance," applied to Hebrew not only Russian poetics but connected it to Zionist nationalist ideas fomenting in Odessa at the time. Bialik's verse seemed fresh, innovative, its diction and rhythms sounding new in a language that had hardly been heard outside the yeshiva. Although the adjustment from an Ashkenazic to Sephardic accent proved difficult for Bialik when he moved to Palestine in 1924, his poetry was an integral part of an effort to use Hebrew as a spoken language. As Jews began immigrating into Palestine in increasingly greater numbers, and the process of reviving Hebrew as a living language gained momentum, poets who had been writing in Odessa, Warsaw, and other European cities faced a new geography, a Mediterranean texture of light and sounds, and as a result had to reinvent the language of 'longing for Zion' and 'exile from Jerusalem' in response to their real encounter with the land.

While Avraham Shlonsky, Natan Alterman, and Leah Goldberg, all born in Russia and arriving in Pre-State Palestine as young men and women, wrote in a Hebrew learned in Europe, they tried to create a natural spoken style. But the writers who followed them who had come of age in Palestine, particularly Yehuda Amichai and Natan Zach, felt the strain in Shlonsky's and Alterman's poetry. Zach accused Alterman of not using the natural rhythms of spoken Hebrew. As Israeli society developed and became more complex, so Hebrew expanded to include registers of language reflecting that complexity. With the creation of the State, the influx of new immigrants affected the language in unexpected ways. Hebrew opened up in all directions.

Both Amichai and Zach immigrated to Israel from Germany as young boys, and were among the first Israeli writers to literally grow up with the language and give modern Hebrew voice to a vision darkened by the Holocaust and continued Arab-Israeli hostility. Their poetry is distinguished by its natural speech rhythms, its accessibility, its lean, elegant style, and its vocabulary grounded in the details of the quotidian. Yet always present are the ancient Hebrew sources, the resonant echoes of Biblical word and rhythm. As Israel experienced new crises, however, and the religious, national and social values upon which it had been established came into question, a new generation of poets, in turn, accused Zach and his generation of not being open to experience, to the world, or to a changing Hebrew in a changing Israel. The "Tel Aviv Poets"—Meir Wieseltier, Yona Wallach, Yair Hurwitz, David Avidan—demanded a more direct confrontation with the reality of their lives: the aftermath of several wars, the burden of post-'67 occupation, the absorption of new immigrants, the shattering of national myths of returning and reclaiming the homeland, questions about religion in a secular society, familiarity with a living spoken Hebrew. And the city that charged their imagination was the city where they lived—lively, quick-paced Tel Aviv. It was time for dissonance, disjunctive syntax, slang—as though the Hebrew purified by Zach and Amichai had to be adulterated and given wider range in order to reflect a society in crisis. No more lyric wholeness or quiet tones, the music now was fragmented, louder, from Tel Aviv's noisy bus station and the imperfect speech of immigrants, part Polish, part Arabic, part American English, part street talk, all that these younger poets felt was missing in the verse of their predecessors. What could be heard in their poetry was aggressive, jarring, startling and amplified; and in the case of Wallach, for the first time in modern Hebrew, it was the female voice of an aggressive, transgressive, at times transcendent "sacred prostitute."

In the early 1920's, several women poets—including Ra'hel and Esther Raab—began to make their voices heard in Palestine. Ra'hel's poems are still admired and sung as popular songs, and Raab is considered the first native Hebrew modernist woman poet, yet the female identities these poets examined in their work were nevertheless traditional, in keeping with Ben Yehuda's urgings. In the late 1960's, an intense female self-perception linked in spirit to these earlier poets became harnessed to a defiant unorthodox intellect in the poetry of Yona Wallach. As one of the "Tel Aviv Poets" beginning to write in the 1960's, Yona Wallach's work came to full force in the wake of the Yom Kippur War.

Born in Tel Aviv and raised in Kiryat Ono, Yona Wallach never left Israel's borders; completely 'at home' in Hebrew, she used its street talk with impunity. As one of the first generation of poets to be "carving the language as native speakers from the inside out,"[1] she exhibits not only a brashness but an exhilaration and garrulousness in her poetry, an unleashing of energy and excitement in the free use of what had in the past been restricted. She lived close to the senses and wrote often of the ruthlessness of feeling. She dared to present herself as a blasphemous woman, shifting from childish innocence to blatant sexuality, as no woman writer in Hebrew had done before.

Yet it is her artistic achievement and the radical uniqueness of her style—the force-of-nature intellectual energy, irregular metrics, broken syntax and the innovative treatment of gender in the holy tongue—that has earned her a place at the forefront of modern Hebrew poetry. In many of her early sharp-edged lyrics, she speaks through personae—children in the grip of pain or terror who persecute and inflict pain on others, wounded and rejected female souls with strange, foreign-sounding Christian names on the brink of madness. Written in the late '60s, these poems approximate natural speech rhythms and primary diction.

In much of Wallach's later work, mostly long incantatory monologues written in the knowledge that she was dying of breast cancer, she expresses impatience and disdain for 'the wrong kind of sex;' charged with heat and tenderness, anger and sorrow, these poems are moved by a courageous and desperate search for love and guided by a deeply religious sensibility:

> Again the soul's too big on me hanging down like a giant
>   piece of clothing
> like clothes the soul reaches my feet down to my shoes a giant

---

1 Gabriel Levin, "By Way of Preface," *London Magazine*, August/September 1987.

like a father's clothing on a little girl the soul hangs down
large clothes hanging down like a soul on consciousness
like a giant soul on a child's consciousness consciousness
     hangs...

                   ("Again the Soul")

Yona Wallach, beyond immersing herself in the immediate and palpable, evokes a near-hallucinatory world of the inner self. She rejects any suggestion of influence from the Hebrew tradition. "I hated Hebrew poetry and literature. It seemed like one big deception. I loved Baudelaire and Walt Whitman. It seems to me that Hebrew poetry misses the point...it conceals everything from us. They didn't speak to us about suffering. They spoke about Bialik, that fat self-satisfied man adored by the entire nation, but they didn't speak to us about madness. Everything was fat, everything was national...I hated Shlonsky and Alterman and all the poetry. I hated Amichai..." And although Dahlia Ravikovich, one of Israel's leading poets, has used Biblical echoes of spoken Hebrew to dramatize personal struggles, even distorting the sacred to mythologize the self, much of her early lyrical poetry is characterized by classical restraint, Biblical conciseness, and female stereotypes. Wallach dismissed her, saying: "Dahlia isn't involved enough with sex. She's not revolutionary enough...She isn't a feminist."[2]

    Wallach exercised an immense linguistic freedom in her command of Hebrew. Just as traditional Judaism separates the sexes, Hebrew marks gender on every adjective and noun, and so grammatically and syntactically maintains that separation; similarly, women in Judaism are traditionally reticent about their sexuality, so the language 'hides' them in the plural, favoring the masculine as the norm. Wallach manages to take the 'natural' dichotomies in male and female sex and gender, and fuse or exchange them. She overcomes the most basic divisions, rejecting the cultural and linguistic constructs that dictate them. She calls the language a sex-maniac, poking fun at the highly gender-controlled Hebrew with both laughter and love in her voice:

---

2 Yona Wallach in an interview with Helit Yeshurun, Editor, *Haderim*, Tel Aviv, Fall, 1984. All the quotes of Yona Wallach used in this essay are taken from that interview.

English has all the possibilities for gender:
every I—in effect
is every possibility of sex
and every you (feminine) is you (masculine)
and every I is sexless
and there's no difference between you (feminine) and you (masculine)
and all things are it—not a man not a woman
you don't have to think before referring to sex...
Hebrew is a sex maniac
she wants to know who's speaking
almost a vision almost an image
what's forbidden in the whole Torah
or at least to see the sex
Hebrew peeks through the keyhole...
                    ("Hebrew")

Yet what begins as a negative comparison between the re-
strictive Hebrew and sexually permissible English ends as a love song
to Hebrew:

look what body the language has what dimensions
I will love her now without cover of tongue.

Wallach's poems are governed by the ear, animated by excited
and spontaneous speech, responding to intense personal needs. Her
father was killed in the War of Independence when she was a girl. She
had herself committed to a psychiatric hospital as a young woman,
taking mind-expanding hallucinogens as part of her treatment in or-
der to observe her states of mind under the influence of drugs. Wal-
lach the Poet-Entertainer at one time wrote for and appeared with
an Israeli rock band. She saw poetry as a way out of the inner chaos.
"I saw that I haven't a defense. That's what rescued me...that's simply
life itself...I don't live without poetry. Poetry is natural bread. You also
need music. But what saved me was the need to understand life. The
thinking about life saved my life. I wanted to decode for myself what

I saw, the riddle of the world. That's the way I wrote my understanding."

In Wallach's poetry, God has body, voice, a physical presence she has known intimately in all the passionate imperfection of human encounter. Simultaneously she stands as if one with the radiant angels and also as a secular woman, a modern poet alienated painfully from her God, in a state of desire and engaged in a process of constant struggle and choice:

> Never will I hear the sweet voice of God
> never again will his voice pass under my window
> big drops will fall in the wide open spaces a sign
> God doesn't come anymore through my window
> how again will I see his sweet body
> dive into his eyes not descend anymore to pull out
> glances that pass by in the universe like wind
> how will I remember this beauty and not weep...
> ("Never Will I Hear the Sweet Voice of God")

She treats what is generally accepted as religious, sexual or national identity as material to be tested, turned on its head:

> When you come to sleep with me
> come like my father
> come in darkness
> ("When You Come to Sleep With Me/Come Like My Father")

What appears at first a shocking taboo-breaking poem about an incestuous longing becomes a clear and immediate expression of desire for God the Father. In a series of love poems beginning "When You Come..." Wallach daringly invites the male to play various social roles of authority, such as Judge, God, Father, and so explores the sexual rules that govern these relations at the same time that she expresses deep personal longings and love. For Wallach there is no separation, no contradiction between the transcendent and the physical; further, sexual desire becomes an avenue to the transcendent. It is only by shocking the system out of habituation, compartmentalization and the mundane, and going beyond society's acceptable norms to the perverse, aggressive, and transgressive, that one can achieve revelation. Like the Biblical word for harlot, "*kedsha*" (from *qadistu*, the pagan priestess of Baal and Astarte who engaged with holiness through her sexuality; related to the Hebrew *kadosh*, or holy), she combines holiness and shocking sexuality. Arieh Sachs wrote, "I think Yona was endowed with the devil's cunning. She must have known just what she was doing when she used the opposites of sanctification and desecration for her personal ends as a poetess–entertainer. Thus she managed to store an incredible energy of opposites that gave her mythical power. This may also mysteriously be the secret of the cancer that killed her. This also explains why she cannot, and never will be, pitied, looked down upon, or treated without respect. Her glamour as a literary star is that of a woman who dared to bet on the entire bank...".[3]

In "Strawberries" the speaker is a man, emphasizing, according to critic Lily Ratok, the stereotypical perception of femininity in a patriarchal culture. The erotic fantasy in this poem is the most refined and astounding in the "When You Come" series: the man requests that the woman, while acting like a small child, be an experienced whore ready for any acrobatics that give him pleasure.[4]

It is the poem, "Tefillin," however, that is credited with demonstrating sexual exploitation most provocatively—even pornographically—and which created a public storm. Wallach's friendship with the religious poet Zelda, so important to them both at the beginning and based on a shared passion for freedom, imagination, and spirituality, came to an end when Wallach published "Tefillin." Zelda refused to ever be published again in the same journal as Wallach, and was heard to say, "I wish I had died before seeing that poem." In "Tefillin," a woman binds her lover in the leather straps of one of Judaism's most sacred religious rituals reserved for men, the phylac-

---

3 Arieh Sachs, "The Marriage of Heaven and Hell," *Modern Hebrew Literature*, 1985.
4 Lily Ratok, *The Angel of Fire: On the Poetry of Yona Wallach*. Hakibbutz Hameuhad, Tel Aviv, 1997.

teries, or *tefillin*. But first she invites him to bind them on her body till she "swoons with sensation." Then in what seems a sado-masochistic trance she moves them onto his body, wrapping and twisting them till she chokes him with the *tefillin*. It is only then we understand that this entire act has taken place in a public setting, on a stage before an astonished audience. The Hebrew word for stage, "*bama*," is close in sound to the word for the central platform in a synagogue, "*bima*;" Wallach sexualizes the *tefillin*, invading that sacred space usually inhabited only by men. Perceived by many as shocking, blasphemous, sacrilegious, demonic, "Tefillin" seems to violate the most basic religious and sexual taboos. At the same time, as a poem of extraordinary force, in language that is alive and uninhibited, it manages to usurp the traditional male religious ritual and sexualize it; by letting the words lead her, the speaker uses it against the male lover in an erotic act of extreme, ecstatic, and excessive power:

> Come to me
> don't let me do anything
> you do it for me
> do everything for me
> what I even start doing
> you do instead of me
> I'll put on tefillin
> I'll pray
> you put on the tefillin for me too
> bind them on my hands
> play them on me
> move them with delight on my body
> ("Tefillin")

It is not only for shock effect that Wallach speaks through voices both male and female, many and one, but by means of shock, to transcend everyday life. Through sexual physical passion and transgressing the conventions of everyday life, Wallach fuses the opposites of the sacred and profane, and makes the physical and transcendent inseparable. Moving at great speed, her poems discourage a detailed, close analysis. Incorporating irregular rhythms and prophetic pronouncements that explode universal sexual taboos and violate sacred religious beliefs, they are often but not always lucid, following their own idiosyncratic interior logic as their spiritual landscape keeps shifting. "I would play with fear/as with a child," she writes in one of her last poems, characteristically combining laughter and anxiety.

The enormous challenge I felt when first confronted by Wallach's work has remained with me; the whirlwind that pulled me in has brought me at times to a place of surprising quiet and light. Often the process of translating began with only a nugget of sensation; I then worked word by word on a poem, frequently encountering Hebrew phrases that gave off signals, hints of Biblical or archaic language, confusions of gender or subject-verb connections raising sexual issues, and the use of opposites—the sacred and profane, Heaven and Hell, male and female—as interchangeable images. Wallach joins polar opposites in sweeping gestures, singing and laughing, at times with bitter humor, only in order to bridge the gaps. As whole poems gradually coalesced for me, and meanings surfaced, many of them nevertheless remained syntactically fragmented. My struggle to translate Wallach's poetry into accessible English continually raised some essential questions: how to render the poems into an English that makes sense without filling in the spaces of Wallach's Hebrew? how to achieve the Hebrew feel of some of her phrases with an English (e.g. "pleasured" in "Tefillin") that does not read like a partially realized translation? Arieh Sachs said that whoever tries to read Wallach's poetry slowly may get lost.

As she speeds along, I have tried to keep up with her, to listen as syntactical fragments turn into whispers or screams, to hear the voice of her mind-movement, to allow the discomforts and the pleasures of her flashes, and to bring the poems to an English that is faithful to her quick, shifting idiosyncratic Hebrew and at the same time lead us to light, a wild light at the end. I hope I have done that.

I would like to express my gratitude to the National Endowment for the Arts for the translation grant that greatly assisted me during my work on this project.

I want to thank Sidra Ezrahi, Zali Gurevitz, Kathryn Hellerstein, Chana Kronfeld and Miri Kubovy for their suggestions, Gabriel Levin for his rare insight and deeply appreciated generosity. Above all, I am grateful to my children for their patience and my husband Donald for his encouragement and support.

Linda Zisquit
Jerusalem, July 1997

NOTE TO THE EXPANDED TRANSLATION

Wild Light: Selected Poems of Yona Wallach was published in 1997. With that volume—the first book of her work to appear in English—I brought to the public some of Yona Wallach's best known and most accessible poems in English translation. Immediately after its publication I started translating additional poems, and continued making changes in the ones already published. It seemed only natural to go on with the Wallach project to create an expanded collection that truly reflects the range of Wallach's genius and courage. In this new volume *Let the Words* I have added many of the more difficult short lyrics and a number of the longer meditative monologues in order to provide a more balanced offering of her work.

Since her death at 41 in 1985, Wallach's work has continued to have a profound effect on the Israeli cultural landscape: composers set her poetry to music, visual artists use it in developing their works, younger poets address her in their poems. She has been credited with freeing the Hebrew psyche, and is often referred to in the present tense as *achshavit*, still having what is called in Hebrew "nowness."

Wallach's Hebrew delights, even as it provokes and mystifies, overturning traditional habits of reading and opening the way to uncharted territory while plumbing the language's ancient layers. Translating Wallach is like a shocking immersion in the linguistic mix and complexities of contemporary Hebrew as well as the sources from which she drew inspiration and ammunition.

But can English take in the eccentricities and idiosyncrasies of Wallach's Hebrew? One of the challenges has been how to decide when to recreate in English the ruptures in syntax and ungrammatical phrasings and when not to, when to smooth over and when to keep the strangeness of the Hebrew constructions. I was faced with poems beloved by Israeli readers that seemed at first untranslatable because of the misuse of pronouns (e.g. "We didn't want") and confusing disruptions (e.g. "Man's way is not like fowl," "Dormition Eye Your Surrounding," "Bambi All of Life"). These linguistic oddities demanded closer attention, and ultimately rendered some of the most satisfying translations. The puzzling elements of Wallach's innovative, experimental writing began to appear as a foundation-in-process for the development of her personal code: "I'm already sick of putting myself to sleep with tender sentences" ("Before Sleep"). Throughout her life Wallach followed a self-propelling directive against complacency, continually daring herself and her readers to rethink their language and their lives through the stimulus of linguistic discomfort. The final poems—written when Wallach was dying of cancer—are, in contrast, syntactically smooth and radiantly coherent.

Perhaps it is a combination of time and improved language skills that have enabled me to approach poems that had previously been out of my reach. I hope I have not been presumptuous in taking on this task. It has been a remarkable journey.

I am grateful to Sidra Ezrahi, Ariel Hirschfeld, Chana Kronfeld, Lilach Lachman, and Zafrira Lidovsky-Cohen for their generous help and support, and to Gabriel Levin who—as always—has been my true reader throughout this project. I want to express my gratitude to Stanley Moss for his fine editorial assistance. Deepest thanks to my husband Donald and to our children Daria, Yael, Tamar, Udi and David for their patience, love, and invaluable insight.

Linda Stern Zisquit
Jerusalem, Israel
March, 2006

from THINGS (1966)

JONATHAN

I run on the bridge
and the children after me
Jonathan
Jonathan they call
a little blood
just a little blood to top off the honey
I agree to the pierce of a tack
but the children want
and they are children
and I am Jonathan
they lop off my head with a gladiola
stalk and gather my head
with two gladiola stalks and wrap
my head in rustling paper
Jonathan
Jonathan they say
forgive us really
we didn't imagine you were like that.

CORNELIA

In the middle of the night the devil
appeared and told Cornelia
this is the time and Cornelia
who lacks initiative and she must
Cornelia and the devil went walking
in the middle of the night to pick nettles
the devil got tired and quit
Cornelia has a nettle rash and she picked
really you might have thought
Cornelia was a red she-devil
in the morning the people did it to her
because they thought Cornelia was a red she-devil
and Cornelia didn't know
she always thought they do it to her
because she is Cornelia.

CASSIUS

The crows call to you
to leave the land and rebuild
you smear your face with the paint of fires
and start Indian howls
but
what was yesterday a candle
things are happening far off
things are happening nearby
someone is blowing up a balloon
and letting the air out
someone is blowing up a balloon
and letting the air out
child poor child
I come to cradle you
crazy girl
I've come to take you home
Cassius my beloved
Cassius my beloved
you will hear crows till the end of your days.

WHEN I CAME TO TAKE HER FROM THE CLOUDS

When I came to take her from the clouds
she was already bound
sounds of the *coo-coo* and owl
flamed in her ear
Pink Julian left
us a twisted web
I knew she would fall
but I tried
I tried
and around me pink Julian wound
a cellophane sheet with a red ribbon

★

I am the holy virgin
I am the holy virgin
Do you hear me
You suffer no more
You no longer suffer
Over.

CHRISTINA

Doing little continuous acts
examining their thumbs
the eczema on their legs
do Ethiopians also have eczema between their toes
joining hands and going out
in a small dance around Christina
for what for what
they wail around her
Christina waits
what's your name Christina
Christina thinks and tries to feel
the circle tightens around Christina
the yearning weakens her
in the depth much play-lay-lay
circling in front of her and making faces at her
her head spins between the wailing
and with a loving tone each one
whispers to her so what.

★

When the angels are exhausted ·
we fold their wings
with pleasure with pleasure
we raise the whip
when the angels begin
we lash into them
until dew floods the earth.

LOTTE

With a monkey wrench Lotte combs
her hair springs
takes pills against different
feelings of mystery
wears a web dress
and just goes out what
Lotte grasps instead of
the truth is you have a great body
so why then a war pipe
but Lotte took pills
and now she understands only words.

★

and that's not what'
ll satisfy
my hunger no
that's not
what
'll ease
my mind
no
that's not it.

SEBASTIAN

About Sebastian
who never existed
not even a form
Sebastian is
a delicate illness with fever
taking pity
I wanted to establish in his name
something to make Sebastian come true
something like
a house of archers
from its lattices you see a pink city
but to think of the beginning
when everything's painted and the concrete's slick
and the blueprints
today I returned from another city
where a Sebastian would always happen to me
and didn't happen to me today
I know about this
more than I feel
I know too that my wonderful porcelain cup
broke and I didn't pick up the pieces
If I'd gone mad I would have built
thousands of tiny velvet carriages and in each one
I would have put a sliver of that porcelain
meanwhile I envision
lakes and rare animals
and a leader of mustangs in whose presence
possibly again Sebastian

ANTONIA

In my opinion Antonia is
the most beautiful woman in the world
it didn't help her much
even the boy Yehoram she thought
needs too many
pills for the storm of his soul.
All the holy young girls
whispered with bubbling venom
how she's drowning how she's
sinking she doesn't really know
and we from the mountains see
Antonia almost had a heart
when the boys knelt at her feet
she was a lot to herself
but Antonia wanted
and the boy Yehoram covered with blood
and Antonia said dew
I know I'm in the Inferno
at least there are sublime voices
she feels how the seraphim lay
on her their hand devils
didn't have to show a sign
when it seems for an instant that already in the sand
and the holy women
and then in the city a voice

ABSALOM

One more time I must
remember my son Absalom
whose hair caught in my womb
and didn't come out for me
to finish Absalom my son
I construct the possibilities of my feeling
compassion floods me
and the possible hunger
the wills of heredity
and Absalom who wasn't allowed
in another incarnation Absalom will be
my lover and I'll sense her trace
when Absalom my lover
is a physical sensation or how my belly
is empty of Absalom my son
an arrangement of stars
falling and a sword striking
the magnet on its heart
a precise feeling:
with what will you fight
and what will the wind
rest upon
where will it carry you
the wind my son.

CECELIA

In the pink plots
Cecelia passed me
dripping blue bells
explain this to me
she asked the man who crossed her way
he explained to her it isn't a wave
she didn't understand it
her brain worked hard
but she couldn't feel it
she understood he lives in it
and she doesn't get it
always I'm fog said Cecelia
and already there was pink above the mountains
always I'm fog in a mold
and when I make an effort
I sense sediments of signs
alongside this Cecilia didn't want
to burden me with exact facts
I knew the birds played havoc with her
that on the sea she would crumble
I want to evaporate said Cecilia
I no longer manage to climb the walls at night
how to be a prism and not shatter
or vanish and reappear as something else
in the mountains the maroon controlled the blue
she finished all the chocolates
and wiped her mouth clean
so the ants won't come.

from SEVERAL MATTERS

1

When I look in the mirror
hallucination of pain
is what it seems to me I see
when the wind loves me
and someone snuggles in my bosom for warmth
I don't know anything but
the warmth.
So where's the fervor I
ask myself the curiosity
turning into concept the tiredness into fact
the night passes, of course the night passes
some people in its passing become married couples
and until the night that returns for all
there are a few things to continue

2

The wind loves me
and the rain too. Bread on the other hand
that's a product for love
I'm cracking up from love

3

A boy who lives with quickened heartbeats
a woman who lives with a different rhythm
in the twilight of hours, amazement
at a new bird a look of
strain for small animals
and a few tunnel men and a few
ladder men—a yearning
I move on to a different yearning

4

If only for the sake of like feelings
let us pass with a gentle motion
and with a diminishing readiness, let us
pass to a place the bird
can identify.
Meanwhile I see the splendor beyond
the cypresses
the clover fields soaked with sweat but
they are fields of clover—what is known
about the jackal is known and people clap
hands at the time music that my ear
isn't used to grabs my ear
I'm willing to try out other concepts

5

Daddy I repress where
you're rising in dust now and how many
people I love in fact
where they're rising in dust now

★

Man's way is not like fowl—an echo,
illuminated maze, deep bubbling,
desperate from acceleration, from each corner, hands
knocking forearm and finger.
With wide heart heavy women, gold,
every maidservant a flower, flowing wreathes
in a tree's ascents, a noisy river, excess
murmuring of a crowned power, flooding
from every face, a different face, from each
wreath after it, not one face, we'll see
a form that's perfected, in a moving picture,
the howl begins, that a trapped person
should not go, in elegant corridors,
a pattern of windows, closed
expanses, surrounded by colorful women
bearing vessels of mourning.

NOT AN ANIMAL AT ALL

Not an animal at all
these outlines in thick fog
foam moving in a spring wind
too lazy to dissolve and preserve sweetness.
Hasty in a valley exposed
shade of flowers in a *chamsin*
hairs rustle butterflies
unbelievable is this girl.
In the nights sun builds
a ripple of glimmer cradling silvery
eyes flowing within and without
not seeing, like at all.

DORMITION TURQUOISE EYE YOUR SURROUNDINGS

Dormition turquoise eye your surroundings
swirls of green light strung like leaves
twined at their edges ascending descending
adorning you with onyx enclosures
sons–to–you stepping in tremor and light
yellow braiding in you fine linen and gold
rye a white spark burnishing outlines
touching not touching your smoothers glide down

OH SEA, SKY

Oh sea, sky, wrap me in mists
blend together with the vapor of my eyes,
your white gulls will descend
to alight fluttering and clinging to the poles
to be live sails on my ship.

Fish will fly cautiously from all sides
like fragments of glass for nuptial luck
let rain come down slanted as if intending
to wash the sweetness of my face in its beginnings
to be safe warm streams.

Oh: soul, wind. I'll swirl round in circles
cool down, chill my warm head
jellyfish will be joined in transparent wreathes
sides encircling as membrane to my eyes
and float like a sign that hints of return.

Capriciousness, lightness, I'll walk calm in melancholy
adorned with pearls like love-drops
seaweed will cover my shoulders like a cloak
even those close to me won't be able to ensnare me
my ship will be described as *one-of-a-kind*.

★

A thick blue remains in the poplar leaves
and a great light rests on the lattices of the rosebushes
two pepper trees entwined in each other's branches
at my age, young when I was born, in my honor
enveloped in a sprayed gentleness. Like their blossoms
dark gold of bees hovers, then flickers alternately
goes out and rises, enters the ornaments
bears a first fruit a whish of buzzing full of a sense
that vibrates and recedes, moves to float on the face
to permeate such a bathing love.

from TWO GARDENS (1969)

CRUEL HEART

Little red hearts
come in rows from sun
land heart by heart on the little finger
of a lean-day older woman.
As one they lift a pinky-heart to ear
and eavesdrop on a clear light cooing:
I am the corner heart. Test of the light
shining from hidden repressed dreams.
Lean-day women of middle age
in dresses of cotton and worn-down heels.
If they remember, and their tears
are a filling for the wish,
they cook dinner from a magazine for evening
buy a new nightgown, for love
niggling time from worn-out husbands
if they don't remember
they hold stingily to a little heart
and give it on a holiday to a girl
so a sweet trinket will sparkle on a tiny finger.

FROM THE ISLAND POEMS

All the distant will concede and come forth
mostly narrow-waisted boys
to me to me for gentle games.
The sun will send circles of peacocks
a canopy of peacocks to the interior of our eyes
as tulle separates a lover from her slumber.
Nectar of flowers for the heads of boys
will yearn for oil in the fullness of days
as mercy will cover the lean in character.

OYOY

Woe Zippora where are we stuck
hard days or say it with penults
seas of straws, like drinking
all the days through a straw with what
bandages shall the night be dressed flowery
and pink at the end yellow and in the day
wow Zippora where are we standing.

AS WHITE

This white will drive me out of my mind
like the unicorn I saw on a tapestry
a pure white unicorn on flowers and leaves
making a virgin crazy with a remote gentleness
this white will yet drive me mad.

BEFORE SLEEP

I put myself to sleep with pretty sentences.
Lovers' footsteps don't sprout flowers.
Sparks falling from the sky are embryos of angels.
And I'm already sick of putting myself to sleep with tender sentences.
Now I want to fall asleep to curses.
After all maybe it's worth it for me to draw from curses.
Maybe harsh ungrateful materials will do me more
good convey so much more craving.
Bitch bitch running wild sweet melody sweet
for a while I've wanted to fuck a bitch.
My bitch under hand I'll caress a bitch
maybe a whore. Be my whore with everyone
for money and with me for free with crying
for free for my love from everywhere
everywhere that I might want, be for me.
In Hebrew there are curses shit. Bridget Bardot
leaning against the wall cursing in Hebrew doesn't
make sense. Curse in Swedish
if so growl like a bitch whore.
Is this what is good for deep sleep
I'll say to you. Before deep sleep there is wakefulness
and that is very good for wakefulness.

SONG BEFORE-I-SLEEP
after Godard

They hint to us that there's different sex.
It's good someone knows about it.
If there's different sex br
ing it here and we'll know it we'll sp
eak openly, there is or there isn't.
For we're already verytired of our wo
men and our virgin girlfriends always
showing us in pictures that real
ly there is something else and also w
e feel ourselves it isn't nonsense.
And if there is different sex in another
world new and knowing women wh
y not bring some here t
o teach our weary women and may
be they'll also open the borders wh
en we're tired and sosuffocating.

BLACK HAND

Sometimes a limb grabs independence. In the name of personality
it becomes distorted jumps or vibrates. A limb like that
is the hands of a pianist, a strangler
and a limb like that is a black hand. Let a particular
limb represent you or be responsible,
you can live in peace and it will worry
about its own existence. A black hand with no man behind it
a black hand frightened children
in no way was it the hand of a black man
and I don't remember a glove being mentioned,
it was a black hand from birth.
And I note: a divine voice, at hand
is the black hand an inner-hand?
Evidence from a film: (when the pianist's hands are amputated
they hang a strangler and transfer his hands
to the pianist who won't play and wants to strangle).
A black hand wandered alone in the world
a black hand with no man behind it
and everyone was afraid a solitary limb
would turn everything into its servant.
If hands could force what on who,
basic content controls the hand with what's darkest in the hand
most hands are not aware of it until suddenly
someone allows himself and brains remember
brains worry it will disappear into legend.

WE DIDN'T WANT

We didn't want to make anyone happy with our love
if someone was suspect to us
as if knowing the secret of our love
immediately we'd get angry and fight.
We tried not to look at us
so we wouldn't laugh or let on to anyone,
and if we knew there was someone who'd be distressed
who'd be pained as if our love was from him
we'd wrestle and hate a little
we were simple and warm lovers
whoever felt it can testify.
We didn't want to include anyone in our love
we never talked that way with our faces
also with our faces rarely
would we hint at our abundant love.
From the start we felt it isn't nice
not nice that we're lovers,
very not refined people clinging
and everything that lovers do with the face.
We were gentle, next to lovers
even those who love lovers
feel they're missing out and curious if
this is really what lovers do.
We were bashful as if we were the first
we were modest and insisted on checking
if a thing like this had ever been heard of
if there had been a love like our love.
We would come with indirect claims
there, this and that, they did for honor.
Not when it came to us were we like that
infrequently we'd talk

usually we wouldn't talk.
We would sleep far apart, longings
we planned to preserve during the days all
the days all our love that wasn't promiscuous
that wasn't evil. So it would be in hiding.
We were naked we were wild.
When one of us is terminally ill
it's a duty to tell everything. You have to tell
whoever sees knew already long ago,
whoever thought we didn't love anything
nothing was added to his honor or beauty.

A GOOD MAN LOVES PYTHIA

A good man loves Pythia.
To my great joy, for were it not so
I'd worry who Pythia loves
and to whom Pythia gives love.
A good man like me is Pythia's lover.
The three of us talk openly.
If not him, I'd be Pythia's.
A while back they hinted she was wavering,
I kept away so she wouldn't hesitate
for why should Pythia waver and regret.
I used to think, if only we were two,
the two wings of Pythia, but
they're both happy with me and laugh.
We always laugh together,
they say happiness, and they laugh
and I laugh too, when Pythia's happy.
Why not, Pythia's glad, and if not,
if she were sorry, I wouldn't come.
Sometimes I'm sorry there isn't more Pythia
like there's two of us, but no
my good luck is there aren't two Pythia
and what I am for one Pythia.

★

And every breath was *oy*
and every breath was more *oy*
and with every breath I turned into *oy*
and *oy* when I turned entirely into *oy*
and hey I am yes I am totally yes
I am yes yes I am full of yes
I am satisfied I am forgiving
I love I am hungry
I am yes I am full of yes yes
and with every breath I was *oy*
and with every breath I increased *oy*
rhymes toyed in me
bells struck me
already long ago *once upon a time I was*

MY FATHER AND MY MOTHER WENT OUT TO HUNT

My father and my mother went out to hunt
and I am alone.
My father and my mother are in wonderful hunting fields
and what do I do.
My father and my mother are hunting now
My father and my mother are hunting serious beasts
They never hunted funny beasts
badgers or rabbits. Ha.
My father and my mother are in glorious hunting fields
and I am bored and lazy.
My father and my mother are eternal hunters
and I am at home. What is a home.
All the past of my father and my mother
is of no matter to them when they hunt
and I too am deposited as a memento
of which there will always be one lovelier.

GOGOL'S DOLL

Sleep, teddy bear, sleep,
I wrote a new song
to my old brown teddy.
Sleep, teddy bear, sleep,
with you I am warm
my clever teddy.
Sleep, teddy bear, sleep,
this is your house
and I am my teddy
sleep, teddy bear, sleep.
You're made of leather
and I of my memory
sleep, teddy bear, sleep,
you have a glass eye
and I'm just wet
sleep, teddy bear, sleep,
for both of us, sleep
and I'll do everything
sleep, teddy bear, sleep.

from PRECISELY

★

You were always in me
sometimes outside sometimes within
suddenly you burst out of me
but look you're not astonishing.
You're so familiar
it takes time to see

★

Now I must admit,
I spoke to myself.
It's not an embarrassment
to speak to yourself as long
as you call each thing by a proper
name. And still I didn't call
by name that unwanted
feeling and I will call it whatever
I feel like and this time Zippora.

★

Spirit of my love, things rotate
appear transparent and disappear in a sense I knew
but the astonishment and her panic don't hold on in life
if only I turned my knowledge as a sense
spirit of my love would stand up like being.
But the astonishment and her panic come like a pearl
or spirit of my love in the color of pearl
appear transparent and disappear in a sense I apprehended.
Spirit of my love, where has the one coming gone
the person here and there and spirit of my love in her time.
Spirit of my love was in my eyes in her color
in her eyes but the astonishment and panic are bad for her spirit,
for my love spirit bad as hints for my love and for me
how lost my head when my love comes as her spirit
like being she was if only my knowledge were like a corner
closing like a corner over the spirit of my love vanishing.

★

I couldn't do anything with it
you hear I couldn't make
anything from it it was in my hands
and I couldn't do anything with it
and I couldn't make something out of it
you hear I could stutter
st   st   what did I want to say
I could feel as bad as possible
(you are about to solve a complicated problem
you will say the right answer
it is the last test and suddenly you)
stand like a small child with a bib around your neck
and say st and repeat the question
what did you do with it they ask where
did you waste all this you had a chance
and you have to start everything over anew.

BAMBI ALL OF LIFE

Bambi Bambi
I'll set up a chirpy land for you, all Van Dyke soft-crowned
and dwarf trees specially for you. A cruel fold in the eye explains
they are an open hand in the grass a thousand years
(a man alive a long time dead–living walks takes revenge)
I'll arrange for you a proper and terrible garden
just don't grow don't mature
in public, a bit tiny, nothing will be approved such as me
Bambi Bambi, dear name, every good portion, to place in you
in honor of a private and wonderful quality. Beautiful drugs not
in you Bambi everything buzzes in excess hidden and otherwise missing
don't steal death with a laugh and necessary terrors
everything is whole Bambi in you already a doe's foreleg
Bambi Bambi chances and quality, large and sad, yearnings
much I placed in you and a little life in my time by my side.

★

My consciousness melting away
like memorial candles on Yom Kippur.
Yona Yona the memory is sweet
but I am alone in time.
Where are all my things
one name scent of old sex
the stuff of reality tends to exist,
I weep and strive, strive and weep.

TWO GARDENS

If raisins grew on you from heel to head
I'd pluck them off one by one with my teeth and leave naked
your smooth white body and you'd be naked, how hard
to feel naked. But there's something repulsive about this sight.
I'll say: the vegetation here isn't awful,
the vegetation here is rippled and sweet, Eden vegetation.
Hearty, tall-built birds so unlike
people, did you read me unprepared
to see an animal? Still nauseated before curiosity
I think, it's nothing limbs nothing bloody
and then I run and see only animals unlike
people. No thorns. Everything soft and sweet.
No pits. We're in an eternal garden. Fruits are replete
with themselves. This garden will vanish and not one plant
will grow like plants in this unique garden.
I'm afraid. I see a horizon. My body disappears and my soul knows
a horizon approaching. There are some awful
common plants, and there are some people, flesh
and blood and growth of nails and hair. I see
them. The earth is flat and small. Flesh and blood is thick and alive
the colors are like existence strong and desperate.
Later we're back in the first garden round and blended.
The sweetness of course isn't like honey or sugar.
The sweetness is of nectar. And 'you are one' is revealed in the leaves.
If we were in the Other Place and I'd say to you 'my lord'
you'd see that I am smooth as oil. Or pearl.
But in this exact garden I am light and you are form.

48

DEAD IN THE LAND

The beautiful one dead was already found in my garden
blossoming, rinsed with golden light and the smell of water
at the level of a pear hole rested a splendid dead.
Paths strewn with bright soft sand
surrounded the grass, I saw everything anew
a gift of a dead rested there and waited for me.
Mediterranean springtime early and rising
quietly, transported me like a butterfly
to where sweet pain broke through like dawn.
And I bent over my unfortunate wondrous
white and his blood a most beautiful circle
tablet of his heart, his neck I loved at that instant.
I was able to lament to sing to freeze
my dead, there are no songs in my blood
the earth bequeathed songs to another dead.
With thanks and tears my beautiful dead
what's foreseen in my eyes I was ready to see
how conditional beauty is like a flash of horror

THE HOUSE IS EMPTY

The house is empty and the trough broken—
Naomi who my soul loved where
did she go. The house is robbed, the cupboards
empty. And Naomi is on her terror way
what embroidery or shreds of embroidery
for her body. The orchards are dry, land
abandoned. Weeds, nettles.
She-donkeys don't trample loose dirt
and Naomi doesn't beat she-donkeys.
Naomi who my soul loved. Water-
fowl and life and Naomi where
is a virgin, who won't revive her, and if only
Naomi saw life in her days
and would still summon joy in the meadow

LOLA

Lola, do you still get what you want
have you gotten all you wanted
do you still want Lola
or what happened to you after you got.

Have you wanted something new Lola
so many years and your voice Lola
do you still want with that same voice.
Do they still want you Lola like they wanted

youth like memory Lola, hushing up,
and beads scatter in a whisper on your skin
what will you wear on that day when

you lean over the first well deceiving time
gulping and babbling pleasure in a voice younger from moment to moment
and with eternal desire disappear in the baby of yourself.

★

How to open a rug
for once you have to decide how to open a rug
it's very hard, to pull by the fringes in their place
so its body rolls in place
or to pull by the fringes in their place so its body rolls backwards
or to roll its body from the front into its place
or to walk backwards and roll the body of the rug towards you
and see the rug form expanding bumping into it from behind perhaps

TO KIDNAP IN THE LAND

I snatch children in case the parents object
I also snatch parents I snatch women
in case the husbands object I also snatch husbands
so no one is separated from a natural environment
but young men how they seem ready
for landscape for luxury, youth are like mistresses
gliders possibilities and all that is in youth
I kidnap like only I know how to kidnap.
Not in the old style. (In my opinion) you need to ignore
to not even know where they live in order to pull off
an acceptable kidnapping here, (strictly between us) no forests here
in the woods of the Jewish National Fund you only have to think twice
to find yourself on a Sabbath outing.
Memories rumors, I'm probably not built for this
but when I hear the news the wind goes out of my sails
and the people kidnapped are not afraid. *The Voice of Israel* calms
    everywhere.
In the Negev it's possible to kidnap youth in the middle of day
bright light but where do you see youth there.
At the start I take note of unexpected buildings
Negev youth are protected and walk around surrounded by kidnappers
    of youth.
And that's why I don't base my pleasure on fear these days I give up
whoever I kidnap doesn't know and that's how I am hidden pleasures
(not only) that I kidnap and I pretend.

★

And the boat sliced the flower bed
on the entire lake erect flowers
the flowers bend and straighten up at once
the boat is surrounded by standing flowers.
In the high waters crocodiles glide
the water clear as usual becomes clean
for an instant a whirlpool and movement of blood
for now the crocodiles glide in silence.
And the earth in the lake has strange mounds
and the boat in the flowers has walls attached
life falling nourishes crocodiles
their round belly like live graves.
At what sight out of deep alarm
did seeing spare knowledge
as it's common to think of sinners and saints
for the crocodiles from the boat at fixed times.

ARE THESE MOODS MEMORY

Are these moods memory
still fine voice of a bird, wings
apple scent giving face to the air
I float in these I don't know myself.

Approaching this and for a moment moving away
like a frost in front of me for the things
and when these festive ones wash the bodies
the name exists in all the things.

Pain and purity are brave like a living person
even if replaced by dark patterns
for all this they remain faithful.

WHERE ARE THE SOUNDS MY HEART LOVED

Noisy decreasing and by my ear blessing,
the inner ear expanding
and these increase trilling shapes of gold over shapes of gold
a sound of seraphs from the rustle of their lives in their movement
a live tune from their turns unraveled and composed.
And the angels of man? Moving compressed, shapeless
from materials too delicate in essence to become monsters
and wailing in their inner voices to the very end of the scale.
And the inner ear deepens to the last depth
the image-voice of cherubs who haven't appeared in man
plays sounds as blood in an instrument's memory.

★

Man accumulates memories
like ants in the summer months
like a grasshopper in summertime
and it happens that man sings
and in winter ants assemble
moving with their property slowly destroying
the property and the winter
and the grasshopper in winter sings to the openings
to taste from memories of the beloved season
that evaded him completely in his song.

THE VOICE OF GOLD AND THE VOICE OF FLESH

The people the people of gold like a kind of machine folk
glow like gold in the afternoon sun and I imagined their heart
heart of gold pumping rushing gold to their brain
gold dust shed from the gold rays of high sun
the leaves and the flowers and all this gold on gold
and the voices were like gold knocking against thin and thick gold
and their actions I didn't interpret for the thinness kept becoming more
what thinness? two fine membranes one gold and one dust
and a momentary–gold–land turned into a place of living materials
life and life and life and life and life and life
and the sounds of flesh that I gave voice to were life and life.

THE MONSTER DOE

And all the birds were in my garden
and all the beasts were in my garden
and all of them sang the bitterness of my love
and the doe sang more wondrous than all others
and the song of the doe was the song of my love
and the voice of the beasts was quiet
and the birds stopped screeching
and the doe climbed onto the roof of my house
and would sing to me the song of my love
but in each beast there's a monster
just as in each bird there is something weird
just as a monster exists in each person
and the monster doe walked around the garden
when the birds bowed their heads when doe sang
and the beasts dozed when doe sang
and I was as if I wasn't when doe sang
at that soft moment she struck my gate.
And all the beasts fled and the birds flew off
and the doe fell from the roof and broke her head
and I ran away and in the garden of my love shuts a monster
gorilla black and evil as oblivion.

TWO GARDENS

And in one garden all the fruits are yellow and ripe and it's all round
and in one garden all weeds and thin trees
and when round garden feels thin garden feels round
and when thin garden feels round garden feels thin
and round garden needs thin garden
and thin garden needs round garden
and in round garden from every fruit pipes go up and down
and in thin garden the signs of direction
and into the pipes come the sounds of the ripe fruit
and in the thin garden there is no sound
and the round garden needs the stillness
and the thin garden longs for a sound
and when round garden feels thin garden
the sound extends to the outer ends of the fruit and doesn't go up the pipes
and round garden lives the life of its forms
and when thin garden feels round garden
its true symbols strike the true fruits and make music
so the thin garden plays in stillness in stillness

from COLLECTED POEMS (1976)

★

And we were like madmen all night lions roared in us
and we were afraid of ourselves as if on top of cupboards because of
　　ourselves
and we were like the shell of a nut on the face of waters raging from
　　ourselves
and no one approached us to see because we were in deepest anxiety

And big decisions were passing through us like long journeys
and decisions were reversed in us and returning to whiten our eyes
and all night we would toss and turn like wounded animals escaping
　　from ourselves
and near us a man was narrating our ways and the signs

And in the morning there was another man next to us half his face veiled
and we were turned on our sides half our eyes black, half white
and we would count with him or after him the signs and we would tell
　　hidden things
and all night we willed our future and held on to our past as frontlets

Pink dawn brought a new disaster to our homes our protector
　　disappeared
like something inexplicable from the so-called powerlessness of the
　　submerged
all was determined at fixed hours it was no longer possible to tell more
　　than a few hidden matters
and we would lie down as one whose world turned upside-down and
　　the futures would stand and wait

★

sub-conscious opens like a fan
still it is a dark horse still not white
the brain floats in me as if on water, a white rose
and on the horizon a few doctors are chanting, *the dark side*
always accompanied me, embodiment of a friend
sounds of her breaking, again the same foe came over me, her finger
a memory of something in me, still a sluggish animal,
wavering, records another life in me, also in love
making of my life another life, but courage and intellect
are competing over me—already beyond panic and its smell
like a killing field inside me, my part like a shriek,
birds preying on carcasses, as if the hour has come
and after that at the same time
my part near the smell she got mixed up.

Menahem, Menahem, like the birds shrieking a great shriek
I am already after that, I arrange panic in me
and life, my memory and my intellect each in its place, rest,
how I started to fear her fear
and how myself I thought for him, and once I was upon a time

THERE THERE ARE

There there are storms there there is lightning
There there are voices and a stone on trees
There silver shines and there there is life
And on the other side they keep silent and hide.

There there are movements there there are waves
There there are hymns and doubling of loves
There heavenly bodies and there they are fringed
And on the other side they hide in the concrete ones.

There there are cushions there there are roses
There they make love there support lovers
There they play flutes for the standing fallen
And on the other side they hide and there is no flowing.

LET THEM COME

Let them come and bring me foods
Let me die but let them come
and bring me treats
Let them enter and swathe me in wrappings
and put something warm on my tooth
and say all kinds of sayings to me
Let them enter and bring me things
Let them stand about
and it will be good for me nice 'n warm
Let them stand
and me myself are forgetting
let them stand here and me myself are forgetting
and yes, let them come and be like two children.

SUDDENLY I BECOME

Suddenly I become a cowardly person
Why didn't I get praise for my courage
And why didn't I turn into a braver man
And where's the standard that was mine
And someone else and why exactly me.

Suddenly I'm a cowardly person
As to what I wrote, my name disappeared. Someone else wrote this a person
brave strong beautiful
And I meanwhile am a small she-nut, floating on my ground pink and round
What is left of me may it be blessed
Forgive the error, not intentional, so what.

★

The house stands and around it trees
And I am not home I am not inside
So many days passed amassing years
All this and I for a while are identified

Later we feel like we're being led
We'll get in there yet we'll find it pleasing
How could we let ourselves become passers-by
When what we want is to be the ones returning

We want to be here really to be woven
We're related to all this even familial
After all we were masters here for long seasons
Whatever there was then our hearts went after vanities.

NEVER WILL I HEAR THE SWEET VOICE OF GOD

Never will I hear the sweet voice of God
never again will his voice pass under my window
big drops will fall in the wide open spaces a sign
God doesn't come anymore through my window
how again will I still see his sweet body
dive into his eyes not descend anymore to pull out
glances will pass by in the universe like wind
how will I remember this beauty and not weep
days will pass in my life like tremors in the body
near shards of touch-traces more shattered from weeping
the form of his motion as he moves enchanting the air
never will the voice of longings pass the threshold
when man will revive like his dead in memories, like being
if only his sweet glance would stand by my bed and I will weep.

★

We were ready for it
it didn't take us by surprise
we always knew it would happen
not exactly this way but something like it
we were educated for it
sometimes we were even glad it was like this
the main thing is something happens
we gathered it in any case
snatches of life and incidents
but only those that fit
the rules of life as we knew
somebody would always want
and a bad ending always waited at the end
we knew it was like that what can you do
we were not the ones who directed this
we just knew the outcome and the future
maybe we should have given up in the middle
on a little beauty and other knowledge
but we didn't find the strength in us for that
even though we had strength to wait till the end
we always found this an interesting point
a gap between dreams and what there is to want
here too we found those same rules
that we knowingly gave life to their meaning
after it we would clarify
whether to be not dead and not alive
or to be some other life
again we aligned ourselves to rules
that's what we'd do that's how we'd live
sometimes mid-way
it was forbidden to call us by our name
we climbed onto some cliff
sometimes we'd hear and fall

besides that we were tortured
it wasn't good for us out of identification
for us it was always good
we didn't even pay attention to it
we were always busy as if guided
and only for the name we opened our eyes
we wanted to check if it was according to the rules
what happened to us in love dimmed our brains
there were rules of little value there
and how similar to our rules
there was ample strength there and warm enough
sometimes we sank beneath our hope
in a state of love we didn't recognize our rules
here, if we say
who will open our eyes
we mean other things
not love necessarily maybe consciousness of it
we grasped it like the soul a machine
little by little we got to know each of its nuances
between love and freedom
we had a long war
woe to us who have such struggles
and woe to him for whom this is a point of departure
and only rarely when they were human
and not in the sense that's meant by it
rather after we would spit out
our being super-human
or when we empathized
when we were less and less godly
and also when we'd write: we empathize,
we were in a whirlpool, alone
till the body was torn to pieces
and still we would dream the same rules
at times we'd fail
about this otherwise we'd cry

for now we're seeking uncommon consolation
and taking pains to understand times
strictly between us though we're still perverts
sometimes a savage joy steals in
everything works by the rules
now we'll find a form to be happy
indeed appearances but for the moment hidden
so lovers won't bother us
and won't trespass our boundaries
and later on when nights fall
when our enlarged hearts are pricked
and we'll be involved with such matters
for days weeks and even years
in the mornings and in the evenings the voice will pass
and we'll wait for it with great awe
parts of our personality will turn out
and something will rise like dawn in the land of our fathers
not without words shall we remain one day
and not without our letters and our questions
and not with the circled look of our cattle
maybe we'll be reconciled with loss
of some of our innocence and say amen to life
and we'll be less vulturous then
and we'll be healthy like our rules
and not sick from other rules
or even in our exposure may we not be naked
man-like then will come and approach our houses.

I EMPTIED

I emptied, I emptied like a pool,
I told you something a woman doesn't tell herself,
then I thought if I were naked,
I tried to reconstruct the beginning, you know
why it happened, awful, I emptied,
I emptied like a pool,
what I could do I already couldn't from the beginning,
what I could have done before was erased, oblivion,
it could take days for it to come back, I don't see,
I'm still not that experienced, a question like that, an answer
back, I'd like to hear from him, you see,
I don't know when such courage will rise in me again,
a moment like that returns, interesting, it's still not on the list,
I was assisted for a moment, then I was turned around, is that returning?
I'm waiting, you're still, like a different I, like the second I.

★

A grizzly she-bear reared me
milk-of-stars was my main nourishment
the first thing I saw
in the days of my life I mean that I remember
was me how can I forget

THE HEART IS SOFT

The heart is soft like the body at the moment of death
life is hard like the body when it hardens
after death
a last yogi attempt of the body
a last meditation with a last and final
concentration
and afterwards the body and the life
like all that disappointment hardens completely

THE FACE WAS AN ABSTRACTION

The face was an abstraction
the only work is the face

to make an abstraction and not from the face a non-abstraction
that is the good work to make a face
for the face was an abstraction
and the face was work
and the blood without abstraction seemed a terribly frightening
    horror, terrible and shocking
a face not abstraction liquid things decayed starved.

And what was face was an abstraction
and all the rest was idleness
everyone loved faces and things and would stare as if not work idleness
and the damages the person caused the environment
when the face was not an abstraction
and the poetry was clarification of matters
pure philosophy clothed not naked
with images and security

and the one who studied was the one who rose
because the face was work
because the face was an abstraction
because the face is the holy work

and man's face fell to a hidden abstraction and at his feet the horoscope
animals resting without faces for the face was the abstraction
and the face was more dangerous than any evil like distraction
and the mistake is forever a rotten fruit of life
and even as it all was a little and small however much the labor grew
like the size of a man who goes down to the world
and a world is at his feet like at the feet of the world's spaceship
at the feet of the man going down
and at his feet the animals of the horoscope resting

the face was an empty space an abstraction a formula
that wasn't broken down into small change
wasn't ground into dust when it was perfected
it didn't turn into a coarse dough
the result of adapting the expression to feeling
and that was the creation
with compassion with love the creation of the word
which creates the world the expression the feeling
was the new standard biology constructed the way feelings create feelings—
a son baby is its capital a large sum a small sum
inherited from a previous generation
adorned with the power of the mind
the understanding as when the face is an abstraction

VAMPIRE COUPLE

They draw from each other life and brain
remain like burnt out
eyeholes long and empty
surrounded by lines markings contours
of what was once life

COMING NEAR

My good deeds a crown of flowers
a wreath for my head like a garland for Botticelli's girl
releasing a good smell grasses
how far (I have gone) that I have come near
to the fountain of youth again there's no distance
between me and the things
the brook talks birds babble
as if the nasty girl didn't shut the gate

INFINITY SPLIT

"How many women have I" he said inside her
the thousand women who peered from one face
"how many women have I" he yelled inside her with amazement

"a man is never alone" he said trying
to commit suicide like my Ronnie "there's so much in
each of us" there's always someone inside you

to me it sounds like a joke "there's always
someone home" says the paranoid to the schizophrenic
"one?" says the schizophrenic "how many everyone am I"

"an additional presence is a kind of feeling of religion" I quoted
all this at various times while splitting from place to places
"how many women have I" he said inside herself
when infinite personalities began
to sprout from the space the inner ether like grass after
the rain like vapor from many waters like drops of
infinite women like infinite years presences
in places in an infinity of times
"in order to do it you've got to be one" said the last

ALL THE—

All the insipid and threatening
the mighty kitchen sink
in the crystal castle
when the moment is stretched over the surface of life
like a stocking on a prostitute's leg
the holy works history won't remember
together with all the works of the devil
the plans the plots the tales of deceit
the lovers like cannibals sitting
and counting the pains of life like victuals
in a labyrinth dark and tangled as my soul
holy spirits and demons released
death picks flowers gently
in life makes eternal wreathes
like fears in the darkness they glitter spiritual
children who live off me
the wizard locks them up in the castle tells
German tales
on the other side I pass like a bridge
the messiah a small child passes beneath me
suddenly there's light out there living children

from WILD LIGHT (1983)

POEM

In a ravine hidden in the cliffs
a doe drinks water
what do I have to do with her
except the cliffs of my heart
except the well of my life
except him, hidden
a doe
what do I have to do with her
except my love.

FEARS

The demons are going out tonight
playing hide and seek
try and catch
the
head of the king-of-demons
the she-spirits will come
then
lurk in the corners
the gold will fall
from above
to decorate
events
from the head they
are going out
those there
to harass and create fear
they evade
from ahead
and
change
into reality
you'll believe
lies
you'll fear
tremble
all of you
not me
not
on my life
on my life
which still remains
for me
I will be
here
brave

EROS

And a whistle was heard
and the blood flowers
began to drip blood
and all the flowers
began to drip blood
and the large crowd
came to gather the blood
and everything dripped blood
and the skies reddened and darkened
and a small child walked beneath them
and the skies became clear and brightened
after they dripped blood
and were purified and became blue
and a giant gold chalice decorated
with leaves and flowers of gold
larger than all the skies
became filled to the brim with blood.
And a golden chalice decorated
with leaves and flowers of gold
to show that the quota was filled
dripped blood over its banks.

★

My body was wiser than I
its ability to suffer was less than mine
it said enough
when I said more
my body
my body stopped
when I still went on
my body couldn't
it faltered
and I got up and had to walk away
and my body after me.

★

This is the rain
that falls on the grass
this is the rain
that falls a lot

this is the moment
that passes momentarily
this is the moment
that passes fast

this is the gap
created between us
this is the gap
created now

this is the soon
that occurs on the road
this is the soon
that happens long ago

so don't ask why
just do right away
and don't say known
and don't stand aside

and don't take from me
what you won't understand
and don't want from me
what doesn't have sex.

DOCTOR OF MORALITY

goes to the grocery
goes to the drug store
thinks what to steal
what's worth taking
doctor of morality
doctor of philosophy

knows what's bad
what's forbidden
what's permitted
doctor of morality
doctor of philosophy

goes to City Hall
goes to the movies
holds out his hand
as high as possible
gets a license in theory
always studying
doctor of morality
doctor of philosophy

goes to the grocery
goes to the drug store
doesn't lie
doesn't rob
doesn't kill
goes to the grocery
doesn't steal
doesn't curse
lends a shoulder
doesn't swear
doesn't break in
doctor of morality
doctor of philosophy

★

If you want a bad place
                    say it
if you want a terrible place say it
if you want a red place
orange
round
or square
if you want a chimney in it
                    say it

if you want a dead place say it
if you want a terribly bad place

leave me a warm message
say clearly cursed place
closed place
finished place

if you want a strange place say it
if you want a familiar place
                    say it

if you want a black place
gray
straight
and also upside down
if you want spilt blood in it
                    say it

TEFILLIN

Come to me
don't let me do a thing
you do it for me
do everything for me
what I even start doing
you do instead of me
I'll put on tefillin
I'll pray
you put on the tefillin for me too
bind them on my hands
play them in me
move them gently over my body
rub them hard against me
stimulate me everywhere
make me swoon with sensations
move them over my clitoris
tie my hips with them
so I'll come quickly
play them in me
tie my hands and feet
do things to me
against my will
turn me over on my belly
and put the tefillin in my mouth bridle reins
ride me I'm a mare
pull my head back
till I scream with pain
and you're pleasured
then I'll move them onto your body
with unconcealed intention
oh how cruel my face will be
I'll move them slowly over your body
slowly slowly slowly

around your neck I'll move them
I'll wind them several times around your neck, on one side
and on the other I'll tie them to something steady
especially very heavy maybe twisting
I'll pull and I'll pull
till your soul leaves you
till I choke you
completely with the tefillin
that stretch the length of the stage
and among the stunned crowd.

STRAWBERRIES

When you come to sleep with me
wear a black dress
printed with strawberries
and a black hat
decorated with strawberries
and hold a basket of strawberries
and sell me strawberries
tell me in a sweet light voice
strawberries strawberries
who wants strawberries
don't wear anything under the dress
afterwards strings will lift you up
invisible or visible
and lower you
directly on my prick.

WHEN YOU COME

When you come to sleep with me
wear a policeman's uniform
I'll be the little delinquent
you a policeman
torture me
get secrets out of me
I won't be a man
I'll confess
I'll break
I'll sing at once
I'll turn everyone in
spit on me
kick me in the gut
bash in my teeth
bring me out in an ambulance
to the future
to the tomorrow.

WHEN YOU COME TO SLEEP WITH ME LIKE A JUDGE

When you come to sleep with me
wear a judge's robe
I'll be the little convict
after all you really love dressing up
for every occasion you have another costume
don't get undressed wrap me in your black robe
and under it be naked
put me in
I'll be the little convict
the mental existential delinquent
the one who sentences himself
to a thousand spiritual deaths a day
I won't live eternal life
I'll die the next minute
without identity like a stinking vagrant
be the law
wear a wig on your huge head
fuck me standing
stick it into me so I won't know where I am
all these games
that only you know, play
otherwise I won't remember it's you
otherwise I won't know who you are
do it so I'll know

WHEN YOU COME TO SLEEP WITH ME LIKE GOD

Come sleep with me like God
only in spirit
torment me with all your might
be unattainable forever
let go in my suffering
I'll be in deep waters
I'll never reach the shore.
Not even in a glance
not in feeling
or in flood
waters below and above
never any sky
open air
the open place most closed in the world
an open place
always an open closed place
not open not closed
that is, closed open
that is, not closed and not open
never shall I imagine
to see everything from above
to see from above the landscape
be only spiritual
a pain clean and alone like the sound of pain
never shall I touch
never shall I know
never shall I really feel
not ever really
like all those of yours
always on the way

WHEN YOU COME TO SLEEP WITH ME
COME LIKE MY FATHER

When you come to sleep with me
come like my father
come in darkness

speak in his voice
so I won't know
I'll crawl on all fours
and I'll speak about what I don't have
and you'll scold me:
"my material"
separate from me
at the gate
say goodbye
a thousand times
with all the yearnings
that are
until God says:
"enough"
and I'll let go
and I won't sleep
not with God
and not with my father
I'll want to sleep with you
but you won't let
together with my father
suddenly you'll be revealed
as the one in charge of
the restraints
my father will be an angel
minister of hosts
and the two of you will try to make
something of me

I'll feel
like nothing
and I'll do everything
you tell me to do.
On the one hand you'll be God
and I'll wait for afterwards
and you won't be the authority
and I just a poor girl
trying to be polite
I'll divide you in two
and also myself
part soul
part body
you'll appear like two
and so will I
like two sea lions
one wounded
dragging a fin
or two women
one always limping
and you one face
and the other hardly seen.

★

Make me a double
someone else in my place
he will love and suffer
live and sleep
yawn and arrange
clean and buy
and begin

Make me a double
someone else in my place
will take a chance and jump
play and fight
meet and set up
and give and send
in the usual way

Make me a double
someone else in my place
will make excuses, apologize
get ready, fail
think and die
and hate and kill
and help save

Make me a double
someone else in my place
who will lay down be tortured
grow things and annoy
eat and change
get undressed get pregnant
and abort

IDENTITY PROBLEMS

Bird what are you singing
someone else
sings from your throat
someone else
made up your song
sings at home
through your throat.
Bird bird
what are you singing
someone else sings
through your throat.

from FORMS (1985)

LET THE WORDS

Let the words do it in you
let them, be free
they will get at you they will come inside
makers of many forms
they'll cause in you that same experience
let the words do it in you
they will do in you as they wish
making forms anew in the thing
they will make in your thing
the very same thing
for they are a thing they will make
understand they will enliven
for you that same experience and its meaning like nature
for they are nature not an invention
and not revelation but real nature
they will make nature a thing in you
like giving a kind of life to the word
let the words do it in you

THE GAZE PROTECTED BY THE IMAGINATION

The gaze is protected by the imagination.
And seeing art as an act
protects all of life

The tongue is protected with pearls and gems
the finger is protected
with a ring
and the neck with a necklace
(like with an amulet everything is protected—a man on a woman—
a bird on a nestling
in my turning over what will I protect,
one self-transformation,
while all this is covered with letters and numbers
emerging in the formation of powers).
Like each thing that's inverted protected
in its magical wondrous inversion protected
by the revolving sword
above the closed Garden of Eden
in the structures of bio-anatomical life
in identical
structures of culture
these for those and for all—

ALL THE TREES

All the trees
have ribbons in their hair
and all the trees
are a little thick
and all the trees
are pretty feminine
and all the trees
are not tall
pretty short
and all the trees
are pale
and for all the trees the pale
ribbons are pink
butterfly bows
in the hair of leaves
and all the trees
smile faintly
so all the trees
finish weakly
what they started not long before
and all the trees
are not sturdy
and all the trees
are not naked
and all the trees
wearing gauze
somewhat pinkish
are also weak
and all the trees
are not strong
and all the trees
without strength
do not come with force
how
not with force

BOURGEOIS

Like any little bourgeois
you're afraid to kiss in the Church of the Holy Sepulcher
you button up a symbolic button for me
and with a scared face look sideways
maybe someone didn't see
how ok you are
a friendly priest smiles at me
sexier than you
with all you have
and more human than you
human is sexy
I lift my skirt with an eye
and show him everything
not true
just a nice day
in church it's permitted and in synagogue forbidden
I'll say something about illusions
pro and con
and you'll button up everything
my sweet Jesus
will go on being human and forgiving
despite everything
so I don't miss anything
we'll walk around cool shady corridors
inside illusions of perspective that architecture creates
who relates to illusions in architecture
where everything's real matter and matter etc..
a spirit will hover over the water
we'll stroll around in the body of Jesus
we'll walk inside the silent waterways of his life
inside illusions that architectural perspective creates
we'll light candles of happiness in memory or honor of something beautiful
and we'll make love wherever you think one should

like any little bourgeois you're afraid to love
living in a dual morality with double standards
not me
first of all I'd go crazy again
little golden angels harnessed to my spirit's feet
bearing me far off high into the skies
honestly start feeling perhaps
warm a cold heart with feeling
call it by its good name feeling feeling
compress it into a few illusions of perspective on the spot
but what will a little bourgeois do to the place
he'll distinguish between place and place
and occupy himself with the original sin between man and The Place
he'll steal little things but not kisses
and won't steal all of life as one should
come let's make a plan and steal all of life
but no bourgeois who distinguishes places
can carry it off
he'll always want to do it
in some other place.

A DIFFERENT BOURGEOIS

A bourgeois pervert
just to spite will kiss in the church of the Holy Sepulcher
with premeditated intention
out of an irresistible
impulse
deliberately
according to a prearranged scheme
he'll make a production of himself
to spoil in the same way
the title of the bourgeoisie
to disfigure its face
always
till the bitter anti-bourgeois end as it were
except for extraordinary cases
that someone set up for him
a sweeter end
like a doll in someone else's arms
with a doll-like mechanical look
on purpose
or not on purpose—
or not on purpose

ANOTHER BOURGEOIS

You make a distinction between girl and guy
sometime later I'll also explain why
example: a girl
is neat like all the girls
and I've met only neat guys
come let's finish I say to you
and I mean come let's finish
like you mean when you say
someone ought to teach you a lesson
why necessarily me
that's definitely a male expression you say
and we do a little work in semantics
all at my expense
someone has to explain to you
why necessarily me
you distinguish between a man and his girlfriend
a different kind of primal sin
where are you at call the imagination imagination
call things by their names
me for example
come let's finish I say to you
with this matter
however much you split the world in two
the world will split you in two in return
the good things you save for the end
use them at the same time I'm waiting
to finish is to come I tell you again
to come is to finish one
with a penis
that's our humor don't you understand?
it's the same thing don't you understand?
at two different times maybe two places
things occur on several levels
and that's our humor
don't you understand?

HEBREW

English has all the possibilities for gender
every I—in effect
is every possibility of sex
and every you (feminine) is you (masculine)
and every I is sexless
and there's no difference between you (feminine) and you (masculine)
and all things are it—not a man not a woman
you don't have to think before referring to sex
Hebrew is a sex maniac
Hebrew discriminates against or in favor
doesn't hold a grudge grants privileges
with an account longer than the Exile
in the plural the he's have priority
with great subtlety and secrecy
in the singular opportunities are equal
who says all hope is lost
Hebrew is a sex maniac
she wants to know who's speaking
almost a vision almost a picture
what's forbidden in the whole Torah
or at least to see the sex
Hebrew peeks through the keyhole
like me at your mother and you
when you were both bathing then in the shack
your mother had a large ass
but I never stopped thinking
the days passed like the fading away of the showers
you (feminine) remained a thin and soapy girl
afterwards you plugged all the holes
sealed all the cracks
Hebrew peeks at you from the keyhole
the language sees you naked
my father didn't permit me to look

he turned his back when he peed
I never really had a good look at him
he always hid the sex
the way the plural hides a woman
the way a crowd is masculine in gender
the way word is male and female
there's nothing like those sweet things
Hebrew is a woman bathing
Hebrew is a clean Bathsheba
Hebrew is an idol that doesn't defile
she has small beauty marks and birthmarks
the more she matures the prettier she gets
her judgment is sometimes prehistoric
such a neurosis is for the best
tell me in the masculine tell me in the feminine
every childish I is an unfertilized egg
it's possible to skip over sex
it's possible to give up sex
who will tell the sex of a chick?
The man who nature creates
before he's marked with a conjugated verb.
Memory is masculine
creating sexes
procreation is the main thing
for she is life
Hebrew is a sex maniac
and whatever those feminists complain about
who seek stimulation outside the language
with an intonation that interprets things
signs only of male and female in a sentence
will give strange sexual relations
on every female a sign on every male a different sign
when every verb and conjugation pattern are marked
what the man does to a woman
what he gets in return

what power she exerts over him
and what mark is given to the object
and to an abstract noun and particles
we'll get a kind of sex game of nature
an emotional event like a young forest
a game of the general forces of nature
from which all the details are derived
general signs for all events
that can possibly happen at one time or another
look what body the language has what dimensions
I will love her now without cover of tongue

A MAN NOT MAN
A WOMAN NOT WOMAN

A man not man
a woman not woman
make love
bare breasts
faceless
sex and face
like in Kabbalah
in black magic
the inside peels off
they lose the
face
a man not man
a woman not woman
in the face a dead feeling
in sex organs
the sensation
the brain filled
with good will
but more
with fear
it's possible to preserve
the emotional
virginity
until the messiah comes
and he will come
the woman will be a woman
the man a man
their faces sexual
and in their organs the sensation
will rise resurrected
a white turtle
a great wall

that came to be from a wave
a dam for all feeling
which breaks up like
a waterfall
to drown
the woman man
and the man woman

I'LL BE YOUR ID

I'll be your *id*
the deepest interior part
I'll play you I'll go wild
I'll make it so you won't know who you are

I will bring to you from the soul's light
I'll bring you to infinity
reveal the secrets of creation to you
be every sound smell taste and form

I'll be your depths
a forest girl who teaches the dumb to speak
I'll bring all the animals around
and call each one by its true name

When you're bad I'll drive you mad
I'll appear as a frightening figure
make terrible faces at you
until you're afraid of your own face

I'll fill your life with hints
scatter signs everywhere
leave tracks in a certain place
so you'll know that I am really for real

I'll take you everywhere
bring you all the sensations
make you hear frightening sounds
show you divine harmonies

I'll fill your heart with abysmal loneliness
it will happen when I no longer am
when you're completely sick of me
I'll disappear as if I never was

The symmetry in your face will change
your face won't resemble itself without me
when you try to attack me mortally
you'll kill only yourself

Then you'll remember the feel the real,
remember everything that is immediately,
draw me close with fear and love
let me be the good things

let me descend at each age
to the age I was in the womb
from there I'll bring you all the visions
if you don't stop me at some number

the alone alone will make a creation
the alone will make memories
the nothing will sink so they'll confess madness
in an appalling irrational loneliness.

MASTURBATION

Again you slept with mr. man not
loving his empty look
and hugged his no body.

Your lover's eyes stare at a strange point
not exactly toward you not in you,
he's young and already so bitter.

The love that penetrated your flesh for an instant
fills your body and soul with heat
from the tips of your hair to your innermost organs,

leaving you again with mr. man not
caressing with no hand your body
that responds with no emotion no expression
on each caress no warmth—

You showed the poem to your young lover
he responds with rage and says it's bad
and not a poem at all and turns his back,
perhaps he thinks he is no man,

he thinks he is no man?
He doesn't understand poetry, from feelings
he demands too much, hours
even five minutes of love is enough
to fill the warmth required for a whole day,
no man chills your feeling freezes
your body, the chill spreads through your limbs

freezes your cheeks and sends a nervous spasm
from the curve of the cheek across to the eye and destroys
the budding emotion and sends a taste of pain
to the esophagus to the other parts of the neck and back.

You explain to your lover the meaning of lovetime,
five minutes are like hours
or even five, there are all kinds, it's worth it
to use all the times whenever possible
for it's impossible before work in the morning
to love for three hours you have to warm up and enough
he catches on quickly and tries but is disappointed
it doesn't seem nice to him too fast time
he wants in more abundance than there is,
but he's smart and there's a chance an opportunity like this
may not return in his short lifetime
you have to change some opinions and adjust to the situation,
but again he's alone with himself and with you
and demands in a light morning the strength of night,

you send a cold glance to no man
and promise to meet him again in the evening
for sure he'll return, he is spiritual death
he leaves the coldest look
and stands beside you waiting to catch each feeling
with hands of air, to turn it into total emptiness into oblivion.

You've studied your lover's look
the two berries of his dark eyes
that might send a glance as tender
as a memory of the taste of grapes, they look with fear
and even more with blind nervousness,
so dangerous to the tender
shoots of feeling and love.

Will he go crazy you ask, will he lose,
the breath's movements on his face show
traces that you interpret expertly,
you give voice to cheerful happy stretching
sounds, he's a partner for a moment throws a smile

and you internalize him with self love
take him out and stare at him as at a jewel,
he emerged from the old poems and he
is one of their heroes, even his beauty's
like that, he is one of the wondrous names
so lost in the terrified anxious
formation in society's womb,
he'll be born from there even more monstrous
he'll be reborn and love you
each morning as he should while he can,

he'll get used to your whoring whose source is internal
and rational otherwise it wouldn't emerge
its decency in every homey respectable perception
that distinguishes between what and how when and where,
and his love will wear fewer dead forms,
you'll still give yourself to mr. no man
in the difficult moments he'll freeze your fingers
stroking yourself with different pleasures,

but poems are just a technical matter
acquired during years of living
the hero will live in every poetic form
as third person or first or second,

he will understand this too
will live as first person, second or third
the impression he makes is mainly that he
lives as third person with himself
speaks about him as about he as about someone you get weary,
speaks separating between himself and his sex
speaks of him as of he and these are not his feelings
that is someone else the sex in general the other
of whom he's jealous of whom he will be afraid,
the sex that's he, he gives it to him

you are his mother you raise him
give him back his confidence his faith in himself
meet with mr. no man and learn about
other people about the other he even
though that he could be all kinds of characters
you attach his sex that was separated by itself
this I feel this I sense this,
I my body my soul myself and my flesh myself,
he'll become cultured will love operas and feelings,
will generalize with more ease about others of his own sex,
because the fruit of love is short of days
so much more than the fruits of a poem like this.

AGAIN THE SOUL

Again the soul's too big on me hanging down like a giant piece of clothing
like clothes the soul reaches my feet down to my shoes a giant
like a father's clothing on a little girl the soul hangs down
large clothes hanging down like a soul on consciousness
like a giant soul on a child's consciousness consciousness hangs down
like consciousness larger than human dimensions descending on a soul
a giant suit shoes inside without sexual marking
a girl inside this whole big thing without answer
again everything's big on me everything's too big on me
like someone's clothes hanging down like a giant consciousness
without sexual markings for a girl a father's clothes fit
without secondary sexual markings for a boy a mother's clothes will fit
the mother's consciousness like a mother's clothes will reach down to her
    shoes on the boy
naked shaking from cold from psychologically naked shame
the introverted homosexual phase like a symbolic garment
till the situation's the real clothing for a given state
the state of mind's the real clothing of a person
all this no becoming our poisoned blood in some measure
all this no was our sense of humor all the no
in fact the mood was the hard part in all the knowledge
kindness is a type of mood a kind of genius
a true mood is real clothing for respect
hypocrisy is lack of style a false mood
a faked state of mind how could anyone not see it
an imitated mood or imitation of mood
in all this falseness how will hypocrisy not emerge as a poison
the colors greens and pinks stream down the face
the oranges glisten the greens soothe and are quiet
me I have no mood I have nothing to wear like
the attending oblivion that ruins the continuous flow of life
uniform clothing that is a good and happy mood
and clothes of ritual and ceremony complicated as experience

consciousness that doesn't discern between life's fine shadings
and the uniformity of state for which any state's good for the mind
will descend as a father's clothes or a mother's on a child who discerns
    between two
ability ah ability like an old man between too late
mood is the true clothing go tell a child

POEM OF TERROR

They cut off his eyebrows
and put him in a room full of mirrors
and he would see only himself
and couldn't shut an eye
and would look at himself with horror
and would look at himself with hatred
and would say every bad thing about himself
and would kill himself psychologically
and would flee to every corner
and bump into himself
till he learned how to shatter and break
and turn things into something else
he would exploit his imagination in every manner
until madness and until smell
would kiss himself in the mirror
and see himself multi-dimensional in the mirror
as if alive
and would curse and abuse
and say every abomination
his soul would dislocate from him
and he didn't know
that his actions preceded his thoughts
and would ask like a child what's more important
nature or art
and art would destroy nature
and all the logic ran with an ability to equalize
he'd sprout a hump
and his teeth would fall out
and his hair would fall out
and his skin would shrivel and yellow
and his memory would forget
and his understanding would be lost
and his origins would lead him astray

and his eyes were open wide with much anxiety
and the mirrors would magnify the reflection
and art deadens him as it wills
as art makes death in him
and each bad thing that was done to him from him
was more dangerous to himself and his flesh
every momentary thing was engraved in him
as always
and all the always slips from his fingers
as a real thing
and all the then will be contracted into a moment
all the always to now
and every this time to the present
once he was enchanted with his evil
once there was nothing
and it came into being out of nothingness
for only the spirit without effort
will do what is called courage
a line goes down to too little life
it seems the body is prepared for anything
for every act of degradation ready
for every mean and despicable act
a soul will remain innocent as if it's nothing
for every intentional wrong and evil offense
it doesn't touch the soul no
it is the same as always it won't change anyway
everything changed already a while ago
but the soul remains itself forever
and as if absolutely nothing happened
it doesn't matter to the soul
the body yells help
but the soul won't pay attention
it won't be blamed anyhow
for whatever reason
it won't listen

will say it's like everyone else
God what a terrible mistake.
Before consciousness became before the face became consciousness
there was no before knowing
before the owner of the face became
before seeing himself
before the face became
the owner of its own identity
he thought the one who will be had died
a child of stars looks at him himself
refuses the face and the consciousness
as if vacating his place to another to his consciousness
his consciousness as if another person inherits
and he had a different speaking voice
and he would distinguish parts from units
so he would have substance as someone else
since he kept it all for himself
he'd explode from his knowledge
releasing pressure within a small thing
and not tell himself anything of this
playing *end of the world* and the endings

TO LIVE AT THE SPEED OF THE BIOGRAPHY

Disintegrating at low speeds
those harnessed forces of evil are released
forces of evil in matter forces of evil in spirit
the intellectual forces of evil that enable
every transformation of matter to be done by them
without averages without descending to some imagined level
without an average the media loves so much
without hands without discrimination against women without
those forces that transform what is not matter
matter that almost isn't except in the world of evil
those forces that are released at the speed of the biography
the biography is cast off like a placenta
a person emerges from a placenta and begins to deal with witchcraft
he separates from it now from the biography
tries to function now without his life from outside
outside himself now he sits in the field and prays
sits in the field like a spirit outside himself outside his body
he'll yet enter his body will identify
with himself he also doesn't identify himself he's not a child
a child identifies with a parent a hero a person also not with himself
pretends he's shooting everything everyone himself
weeps for himself envisions his own funeral
sheds tears like rain or not even that
in one of those situations where nothing seems to happen
he doesn't identify with himself he hallucinates himself
he's outside his body his body appears vulnerable
he looks at himself like a stranger maybe an acquaintance
a moment passed another moment passed, already? He remembered
another voice spoke from his throat not his another's
he spoke with the voice of someone else for some time
with the voice of another small child he remembered
places reminded him places didn't make him forget
he made himself forget slowly repossessed himself

again accepted himself this time he'll be careful not rush
he'll live at the speed of the biography will guard
his soul will say calming coherent things
he'll invent for its sake all the images as they are
without lies only pure exhilarating images
he vowed all the vows and took it all back in Christian fashion
he'll turn into all the religious people he's wanted
he'll speak only with his voice always be himself
won't accuse won't judge will love strong and yet
be free as he was born he's lucky he remembers
others were killed inside themselves at an earlier age
not him he remembers the moment of dying
he remembers the moment of resurrection and precise moments
he'll do his best under the given conditions
without favors without connections without waiting too long
without me my life is impossible he said to himself
and after all everything a person desired, his life.
In the letters woven together into carpets of life
a letter or code or existential knowledge
that will tell him something something really about him
something really known about him the principle of his life's dynamic
the principle of his life force something really about him
to live faster than the speed of the biography
to live slower than the speed of the biography
early on it's still possible to call things by their names
soon it will all disappear in darkness will be lost in oblivion
memory loves daylight—the senses night

TO SEE LONG LIKE EL GRECO

To see long and pretty and polished like El Greco
or to see round and dismantled and not pretty and weak
to see spread out and fat and dismantled and pieces
or to see whole and all and uniform and in colors
and what is unknown to see as circles
alarming all the concealed unknowns
to loosen from the expression any other framework
and to know everything about the other expressions
to see narrow and long and pretty like El Greco
what is the face of things really
what is the face of things for one who has lost all knowledge
what is the face of things for one who has acquired all knowledge
what is the face of things really
to see long and narrow like El Greco
to see nice and desirable and Gothic
not to think like Allen Ginsberg that everything is delusion
not to turn neurosis into ideology and end up with agitation

The feeling of the possible potential is pressing
it is only potential it is not real
it's not in truth that everything is relative
and it's not truth the uncertainty
it's absolute the situation in other words the factor doesn't change
and it's not true that the truth is partial
that the pain is my portion
that the suffering is my portion
that the happiness is not full
that the wisdom is partial
the foolishness is partial

The retarded one makes awful faces
the face of the madman is awful like the face of his son
the consciousness is the children

130

as much as we are vegetative our children are seeds
the consciousness is our children
my consciousness is my future child
growing as a psychotic physical vegetable
a vegetable is one thing one flavor
man is all the tastes all of them all the feelings
all the possibilities
the wise man internalizes eyes with care
fruits of the Garden of Eden are rotten with a taste of the mad
fear dissolves or crystallizes into pains
bursts fear body life as something real
activity for leisure fear as a free inheritance
is made as a sort of object fear travels in the face as if alive
is made generous all of it attributes of itself in live structures

----

from APPEARANCE (1985)

HOUSE SAID THE HOUSE

House said the house
tree said the tree
landscapes said the landscapes
man said the man
God said God
what said the what
meaning to said the meaning to
seeing said the seeing
talk said the talk
I said the I
you said the you
love said the love

what did the house say to the tree
what did the tree say to the bird
what did the landscapes say
to the man what did the man say
to God what did God say
to the love what did the love say
to the directions what did the directions say
to the talk what did the talk say to the I
what did the I say to the you
what did the you say
to the landscapes what did the landscapes say

COME TO ME LIKE A CAPITALIST

Come to me like a capitalist
I'll be your laborer
boy will I work
work me to the bone
you, don't pay me
take everything away from me
mess me up in debts
I can't get out of
I'm a serf
you a feudal lord
pay me in goods
and take them away from me
with tracts of land
you'll give me to give back
what emotional
land
expanses of wilderness
that I won't make bloom
everything will be yours
you won't concede a breath
a soul
living space
personality
leave me a little personality
just a little
so I'll feel bad so I'll know
don't be egalitarian
not my friend
not a communist
as it isn't written anywhere
as it never was

BIRD

One bird sang
but not her song
another bird sang from her throat
sang a different song
the bird didn't recognize
didn't know it was a different song
someone else speaking from her throat
she always thought it was she
in the beginning she was a bit afraid
afterwards not even that
she became indifferent
flighty and flippant
how much? As if she were the one
who made eyes at every passerby
without any identity
but she didn't connect with anyone
for she didn't have her own voice
her voice flew freely
and spoke from another throat
who also didn't know
that someone else was speaking from his throat
an other
and he didn't care either
became flippant
and his voice also flew away
and spoke from another throat
and so on
and so on
each voice
spoke from every other
throat
and no one
knew
who he was.

TUVIA

The earth whispers
Tuvia
the earth approaches
to see you up close
Tuvia
how you look
Tuvia
the earth whispers
the earth comes near
Tuvia
the earth murmurs
I have something to show you
Tuvia oh oh
Tuvia ohohoh

come let's count leaves together
come let's count the stars
come let's count the clouds
come let's count the elements
Tuvia
the earth whispers
let me just come near
Tuvia

the earth comes near
run away
it's not terrible
what happened
run away
it's not terrible
come let's count the elements
come let's count blowing leaves
come let's count leaves together

come let's count how many there are of everything
come let's count the grains together
how many there are in each clod

Tuvia
the earth approaches
to see you up close
Tuvia the earth is a grave
look at it with the eyes of a gravedigger
the earth is dust
look at it with the eyes of oxygen
Tuvia
the earth is home

Tuvia
the earth is no place

come let's count the people together
come let's disturb their sleep
Tuvia
Tuvia
come let's count the hairs
come let's count the directions
come let's count the places
come let's count houses
the houses

INSPIRATION

It's the white god
the white speech
and the white donkey
the white heart
the white tongue
the white emotion
specific
to this moment
it's the white turtle
it's the white deed
the whitest deed
not the white person
the whitest deed
but no
no no no
it's the white mist
it's the white vision
it's the white of the utter inspiration
the freedom that envelops in a thick white
it's the white joy

WERE YOU ABROAD

Were you abroad?
No.
Abroad came to me
I say to her
Hi Abroad
how are you
she tells me about herself
and I tell her
about myself too
Does she want to hear?
Yes, she's very interested
she speaks in Hebrew
and afterwards I
say to her stop
enough for today
come tomorrow
and tell me more
Abroad comes to me every day
talks to me in Hebrew and so do I
everywhere the same language same stuff
like people who get it

THE LIFE YOU HAVE

The life you have
is the life you lived
look back with understanding
find the point of genesis
the creation
create yourself
it's the best world
the only one
you could create
all this is found in you
discover it
begin from the beginning
look upon your life
as a bad lesson
on what was
as punishment
being suspended
standing in the corner
a knockout in the first round
make amends
as one who got better
as one who got sick.

WOMAN CROCODILE

His jaws are the spread of her legs
her navel his eye
he can be anything this crocodile

I HAVE A STAGE IN MY HEAD

I have a stage in my head
and it's more real than any stage
and when I step down from it
I hit rock bottom
I have a whole theatre in my head
and I'm the hero in it
and when I turn out the lights
I'm finished
and when I stop acting
my life stops
and when I lower the curtain
behind my lashes
all my friends
my loves are lost.
My memories
my colors
my magic
my panic comes
my anxieties
my corpses
my insults.

THE WOMAN BECOMES A TREE

The woman becomes a tree
here her two hands arms
raised to the sky
the two branches split
from her body
from the trunk of her body resting
on invisible knees
she is seen up to her knees
her thighs are
roots of soil
her seductive stomach a concavity
hollow in her belly trunk
her abundant hair
long boughs
branches
here the woman becomes
an ancient trunk
she is so pretty
and complete
I didn't see her
before
but I knew
this is the woman
who turned into a trunk
no green leaves
no sign of growth
everything dried up long ago
the pretty face woodened
all is uniform
did everything happen at once
without process
what is impossible to do
from the living

happens in vision at once
what is possible happens before
hand-work later
there's no point
after all it's only the sensation
that creates such an image
I know well who we're talking about

IF YOU GO TRIPPING ON LSD

If you go tripping on LSD
remember me
who never came back from there
I'm still there
facing the window
the red guillotine can be seen from it
my head's about to be chopped off
I'm still there
waiting for the next moment
the anxiety of all existence
descends on me like the slaughtering knife
threads of blood
still twisting down from towels
to the sink
there's no control over blood
you should know.

MY SINS

O bonny look at my sins
one by one they rise like endless children
rise in blue caves bearing candles and lanterns
where will they all go from where do they return
one storm will go one storm return
my feeling will go will yet return even if it goes backward
O my builder look at my sins all of them
like endless children they'll go they're all sweet
will my remembering go on its way and still return?
return like me, child, forever from me to myself
so I'll remember me for the first time so me I'll love
I am the happiness I'll build here with not much toil

UNFINISHED LOVE SONG

Your unconscious loves me
I don't get along with your conscious self
your conscious self fights with me
your conscious self wants a separate apartment
but I love your unconscious
that's afraid there won't be enough
that there won't be left enough enough
that there isn't enough for tomorrow
that there won't be another time
so worried the unconscious
that there aren't enough kisses
and there aren't enough caresses
and is certain we don't in fact love
or it doesn't love or can't
instead of being happy that it loves
it looks at me in the middle of the night
looks at me with a strange look
refuses my extended hand
looks at me as if it discovered or said
something no one ever heard of
something and delays everything till tomorrow
the first and last utterance
don't surrender to your conscious self
I want to be your home
afterwards you'll converge
your unconscious all red zigzags
your conscious self all green zigzags
in twos the zigzags almost connect
then turn and separate into other conscious selves
other states of consciousness
mysticism and metaphysics coming and going
intangible things
memory travels quietly at midnight

meets another traveling quietly
a round happy countenance with a golden contour
I'm in third place in memory
after a long line of digits and numbers
one of the closer numbers
touching other places in the heart
from afar a place touching a place
by invisible and hypothetical means
for visions with a self-conscious outlook
visions with a sharper eye
visions whose view is completely otherwise
all the appropriate expressions create a world
emotions and strong images
experience is an absence of concern
if said directly in words
abstraction is lack of restraints
problems such as too much hair bad odor
are more dangerous than birth defects
for anyone with a sense of superiority
aesthetic cleanliness is the tool
for doing things as they should be done during surgery
Pasteur was a clean physician
every kind of dirt is criminal
your unconscious almost loves me
your conscious self pretends for my weakness
tests me collaborates with suspicion
perhaps when we grow up without restriction
in a restricted time
we'll know who you are and who I was
my strength will be my helplessness
and you'll be sure there will remain for tomorrow
enough caressing and kissing for tomorrow
you won't lack as they increase
and every freeing of another inhibition
will ensure the original progressions

errors will decrease by a legal order of magnitude
as they grow greater in an agreed order
and added up immediately as a negative criminal revelation
meaningless content and empty words
and not only fear of heights or some other
let me try something bad again make an announcement
not to forget to tell you I came out in one piece
how will it end what will you say tomorrow
will your conscious self permit loving me
will your unconscious be secure in the end
or what would you say if
if I were to tell you that
after all when I am you
and how would I do that you
end of an imaginary effort and fictional calculation
how everything would be done
and what would have happened if
and how you would react if

ALL THE EXCITATIONS REBELLED IN ME LIKE SLAVES

All the excitations rebelled in me like slaves--
I placed a barrier before them
tortured them behind prison bars

denied them food for the imagination
and I would take
without a picture of the feeling
without heart

would love without a picture of his face
without the emotion
your end is that they'll jump on you from inside

they'll move in you with force everything you didn't want
they'll break out of you from the inside
abandon you suddenly without

from SELECTED POEMS (1992)
(posthumous poems)

THE ISLANDS OF LIFE

I found
the current to the islands of life
and also sailed towards it
among golden-lit gardens
and visions of terror
that I turned at once in my favor
girl of pictures
girl of visions
creatures from that world
protected me
I built my home among them
as a creature from another world
and anything you tell me about the radiation
won't bring me any harm.
The opposite—
will do me good
will take me from among the weeping.
The mighty flow of the white and black
pearl islands
and again I'll talk in the exclusive language
of heavenly creatures
who transmit pictures to each other
and silences
and see it all in pictures
and know.

★

I went to the one who offered me more life.
I went to God
he offered me all of life
I wanted more I wanted all of life.

OUTSIDE THE BODY

The hypnotist was here
she spoke of the body tired from all the years
serving and doing things for us
and I went out from the body
and sat on the edge of the bed
looked at it
and climbed up to lick it
stroke it
take care of it.

IN A STRANGE NEST

The cuckoo lays eggs
in a strange nest
everyone will know
a crow in a cuckoo's nest
isn't a cuckoo

and I
if I lay an egg
in a strange nest
who will know
that it's a Yona.

And if a man
lays an egg
in a strange nest
who will know
what is a man

and if a man
finds a strange
egg in his nest
how will he know
whose egg.
Whether his
or a stranger's.

And if they try
to ruin your
life
how will you know
who is ruining
yours
or another.

THE MAN WITH THE SPIRIT

Bound up in a giant matchbox
he frees himself
and I flee
he'll get to me
I groan
and twist everything around
I'll act as if I didn't know
I'll act as if he harassed me
it'll work
I'll stick him with a complaint
they won't know I knew
he'll be found guilty
and even if I summoned him
and even if I knew that we would meet
he'll be found guilty

he wanted me so bad
the man with the spirit
grabbed me by the hair
just as I thought
harassed me
I acted as if
I didn't know anything
the man with the spirit
he'll be found guilty.

GOOD EYE

A deer on a boulder stands
and between its two antlers of ivory
a golden star glitters
its body is woolen and brown
and its chest white
and an evil eye
suddenly will come from the left
pounces from the void
and the black like a strip of sky
like a hand
there's no beauty here
only great fear.

NOW LEALEH IS SCARED

Now Lealeh is scared
she's just that age—
the spirits that extend a hand
from the grave and attract
a live person pull her,
Lealeh is seventeen
all the fears speak
her young heart that knows
anything can be:
at a séance a hand remains
on the table an amputation from
the ghost, the daughter
emerges from a small box
and talks to the father
twenty spirits inside the curtain
that blows the mystery of the universe
and tells a story
about the things
that can happen within our power
without our knowledge and with our knowledge,
the powers that hold her
Lealeh's afraid now
of everything
her mother laughs
everything can be prevented
the cynicism of the age and the thought
the maturing mind that knows one thing
that everything's within his reach and he's calm
and I with her am afraid
reviving ancient spirits
and old fears from the hideout
and again for everything there's no reason
and the world isn't concentrated around me
I am outside knocking knocking
and anything can suddenly happen.

COLORS GOING OUT

The colors had a special radiance
and they left the objects
and stood in the room
a half meter more or less
from the source of the color
only now I thought
they're replaceable
in other words—changing

IN MY SANITY

I was afraid to be hurt
I thought they'd forgive me
I passed way up from there
and thought again
about something symbolic
that will pass between them and me,
the armies fought beneath me
and I called for the heads of states
and argued with politicians
I was right,
it was pleasant for me to be convinced
of my sanity.

I NO LONGER REALLY LOVE BEING AFRAID

I would play with fear
as with a child
wave it in front of me
look at its face
and call it
fear fear come,
I would read
the most frightening
things,
I would become addicted to the sensations
as if that were the only thing
still me
the fear,
small fears didn't interest me
only the large fear
sweeping everything away
now I no longer really love being afraid
I found myself sitting
and calling it again whispering
as it was then in those days
fear fear come
come play fear with me
I thought that was
what I had to do
then in those days
being afraid,
I'd freeze from fear
see terrible things
also hear
one day it began
I discovered the fear
I discovered other things
madness for example

but that's in another place
in a similar form,
I discovered the human perceptions
I found interpretation shock later
different things I understood
and other things I became fed up with
but the fear was last
I walked long corridors
always long corridors
of monasteries hospitals
public buildings
and I said to me
that from the start the fear and the madness
I'm leaving I'm fed up
again I no longer really love being afraid
now is the time for reaping
I'm gathering the fruits of fear
mostly rotten
looking at them with a smile
not horror
and rejecting them from my sight
again I no longer love being afraid

ALL

One bird
revealed all my secrets
and I fed her cheese
and I fed her
brown cheese cake
and she flew off and she'll return
one bird
revealed
all my hidden secrets
and she'll scream them out loud
and I wanted
everything for me
everything secret
everything.

NOT FOR ME

I was afraid to be hurt
I could have stopped
between the rows of thick trees
and crossed over the fence
I was afraid from the very moment
when everything
was not symbolic at all,
bright light
washed over blue uniforms
and gold ornaments
spots of lipstick
on the many uniforms,
childhood girlfriends
came to my side,
symbolic moments
presented in brief,
the transparent house
way up from there
and the lack
was real,
not for me
I did all this
that was completely clear
not for me.

★

I don't feel
how I write
it's like fainting
I have no flesh
and I have no bones
and I have nothing
and just this alone
as if I were the poorest
and the richest
and this is the gate to every condition
awareness, it must be, the necessary freedom and the I that is.

AND I BEING MYSELF

Everything is within the framework of reality
I told her
everything within the safe recognizable borders
of our basic realities
that's what complicates the whole thing
and that's its magic
there's nothing outside of life
here and now.
"And the immortality of the soul"
she asked
and I told her
none, that's it, that's the point
everything is here and now
here is the immortality of the soul
and here are the incarnations and the identity
and I being myself
and he himself

★

the oyster of the feeling wrapped
the grain of the I
with a plating of pearl
and didn't feel anymore
and her heart is impermeable
sealed
and the I of her is not
to be touched
such is she
that I know
by the I which lives within me
I will come to her
and I will go.

★

Place a large dam
by the wellsprings of the pain
gather with it
like water
watch over it
so it doesn't disperse
for it is your life.

JONATHAN: *Yonatan* in Hebrew, i.e. *Yo(Ya) - natan* = God gave or *Yo! natan* = wow! gave or *Yonah-tan* = Yona-jackal, or, more suggestively "Yona gives" since Wallach chose this poem to appear as the first poem in several of her collections.

Jonathan, or *Yonatan* is the name of several Biblical characters, the most popular being the eldest son of Saul, the first king of Israel (I Samuel 14: 1). At the beginning of Saul's reign, during the revolt against the Philistines, Jonathan was already a commander in the army. He was a friend and constant companion of David, and assisted him when David was forced to escape Saul's wrath. It is written in the book of Samuel, after the Philistines had fled from a difficult battle with the Israelites, that "Saul adjured the people, saying, Cursed be the man that will eat food until the evening, until I have been avenged of my enemies. And the whole people tasted thus no food. And the men of all the land came to a forest; and there was honey upon the surface of the field…behold, there was a stream of honey…but no one put his hand to his mouth; for the people feared the oath. But Jonathan had not heard his father charging the people; he therefore put forth the end of the staff that was in his hand, and dipped it in a honeycomb, and carried his hand again to his mouth; and his eyes became clear…and Saul asked counsel of God, Shall I go down with the Philistines?…and He answered him not on that day…and Saul said, Draw ye near hither all the chief of the people, and know and see through what this sin hath happened on this day…if it be in Jonathan my son, he shall surely die…And Jonathan told him, I did but taste with the end of the staff that was in my hand a little honey: lo, I am willing to die…and the people said unto Saul, Shall Jonathan die, who hath wrought this great salvation in Israel? This shall not be: as the Lord liveth, there shall not fall one hair of his head to the ground: for with God hath he wrought this day. O the people rescued Jonathan, and he died not…" When Jonathan died together with his father and two of his brothers in the battle at Mt. Gilboa, David lamented their death in a moving elegy. David's love for Jonathan has become emblematic of bonds that transcend death.

Lily Ratok, an Israeli critic, hears in Wallach's lines "a little blood/just a little blood/to top off the honey" not only the Biblical Jonathan, Saul's son, who unknowingly defies his father's order not to taste the honey of the Philistines and is rescued by his people, but also Jesus, alone and chased by many, who agrees to their "pierce of a tack." The phrase *l'kinuach*, literally "to wipe up" is an expression also used to mean "for dessert." I chose the idiomatic "to top off the honey" for its succinctness and sound, rather than the longer 'for dessert after the honey,' or the logically dissonant 'to wipe up the honey.'

A third echo in the Israeli/Hebrew ear is *Yonatan, ha-katan*, a nursery rhyme about a little boy who climbs a tree rather than go to school: "Jonathan/the little one/ran to school in the morning/he climbed a tree/looking for chicks/boy, is that rascal in trouble/he's got a huge hole in his pants!"

All of these culturally significant "Jonathans" resonate in the Hebrew of Wallach's poem.

ANTONIA: dew, in Hebrew, *tal*, also a boy's name

ABSALOM: *av-shalom* in Hebrew, meaning father of peace; in this poem Wallach uses the word 'be reminded of' (*le-hizakher*) and later 'her memory/trace' (*zikhra*), playing on the problematic association in Hebrew etymology between memory (*zikaron*) and maleness (*zikhar*) or malehood. Hence, "I must re-member" seeks to render that connection between 'her trace/memory' and 'her malehood.'

NOT AN ANIMAL AT ALL: *chamsin:* dry desert wind (wind of fifty days)

DORMITION (Dormi Zion): a domed church in the Old City of Jerusalem; a grammatically idiosyncratic poem; through a series of transporting images it gathers a glimmer of coherence.

OH SEA, SKY: jellyfish (pl.) or medusae; *meduzot* in Hebrew; one-of-a-kind: *'had·paami'* is literally 'one-timeness' and used in common discourse to describe disposable paper-wear, diapers, things that are thrown away after one use.

CRUEL HEART: "lean-day" (*d'lat yom* literally means 'thin day') plays on an idiom (*c'shat yom,* literally 'hard-day') which means impoverished and brings to mind the emptiness of her days. I've chosen 'lean-day' for the sound of the simple words, broken by a hyphen, conjuring up both empty and difficult.

OYOY: *Oy,* an exclamation used by the biblical prophets, as woe! or alas! *Oyoy,* a double "oh no" or "woe is me;" *penults:* emphasis on the penultimate syllable can change the meaning of words in Hebrew, e.g. *yamim' kashim'* means hard days; *ya'mim ka'shim* means seas of straws. It is also through the emphasis on the penultimate syllable in the word *Zippor'ah* that we know it is the female name *Zipporah* and not the feminine form of 'bird' which would be pronounced zipporah'.

AND EVERY BREATH WAS OY: *oy,* an exclamation meaning woe! alas! ah!

BEFORE SLEEP: *Lifne shena* can also be read *lifne shana,* "a year ago." "Bitch bitch running wild sweet melody sweet;" *Calba calba mishtolelet neima neima:* literally, 'dog (f.) dog (f.) running wild pleasant (f.) pleasant (f.)' *Neima* (fem., pleasant or sweet) also means tune or melody. I combined them for the rhythm and to include both meanings since Wallach's poem examines the effect of curse words and song on sleep and wakefulness.

SONG-BEFORE-I-SLEEP: "Bring it here and we'll know it": allusion to the horrible group rape and murder of the concubine from Givah. The crowd wants the host to 'bring the man out' to them so they'll 'know' him (*Judges* 19:22) but he gives them his concubine instead.

BLACK HAND: a strange poem with awkward gaps and eerie film-clip images; Wallach uses idiomatic phrases that employ the word 'hand' (e.g., *al-yad,* next to, *ba-yad,* in hand).

WE DIDN'T WANT: "we tried not to look at us" The expected reflexive pronoun phrase would be 'at ourselves,' i.e. "we tried not to look at ourselves," but Wallach's use of *alenu* in *hishtadalnu lo lehabit alenu* instead of *al-atzmenu,* etc. has a childlike quality. The word face, *panim,* also appears frequently in the poem, but rather than in the usual complex expressions, e.g. *bifnim,* inside, Wallach uses face in the simplest way, to mean what appears in the front, *b'fanenu:* "we never talked that way with our faces/also with our faces rarely/would we hint at our abundant love."

A GOOD MAN LOVES PYTHIA: Pythia is the name of the oracle at Delphi. "One" (*echat*) in the last line is a combination of masculine and feminine as well as an echo of Esther Raab's revolutionary sexual politics of the 1920s. The last line of one of Raab's most well-known poems is "*b'echat.*"

GOGOL'S DOLL: It is ironic that this poem (with music by Shimon Galbetz) became a children's lullaby and was performed in the "Israel Festival of Children's Songs" in the late 70s. The poem uses material from Tomaso Lendolfi's story "Gogol's Wife" which tells of his intercourse with a rubber doll.

from PRECISELY: *Zippora* (tzi-por-ah´) is the feminine form of bird; it is also a female name (tzi-po´-rah), Moses' wife was called *Zippora.* Wallach uses this name in several of her poems to signify a woman who is limited or stuck (see *OYOY.*)

BAMBI ALL OF LIFE: a poem of consistently confusing syntax and ruptured phrasings, yet held together by an interior dialog with its own compelling rules and cohesions.

TWO GARDENS: the first fifteen lines of this poem are in the feminine voice, and then almost without our noticing a male voice says "I'm afraid." It continues till the first voice returns with "Later we're back;" though there are no clear gender markings till "and 'you are one'" and that phrase itself echoes the *Sh'ma* prayer so it isn't a clear indication of a male addressee. Only in the last two lines when she says "and I'd say to you" and "you are form" can we be certain it is again a female speaker. I have used italics to indicate the second voice.

DEAD IN THE LAND: *met ba'aretz* is "dead in the earth/land," or "dead in The Land" or "died in Israel," since *aretz* not only means earth or land, but also refers in common discourse to the specific *Land of Israel* (see "Were You Abroad").

AND WE WERE LIKE MADMEN: frontlets, in Hebrew *totafot*, meaning phylacteries or prayer-band, as in the daily prayer, "You shall bind them as a sign upon your arms and they shall be as frontlets between your eyes."

SUBCONSCIOUS OPENS LIKE A FAN: Menachem, a man's name, also means comforter; Yona Wallach's editor was Menachem Perry, whom she is allegedly addressing here. Life: *haim*, also a man's name. "The dark side:" *sitra achra* in Aramaic, meaning 'the other side,' the Devil; in *Kabbalah*, Satan's camp.

INFINITY SPLIT: The word 'face' (*panim*) is always plural and most often feminine. What is unusual here is the reduction of *panim* to singular masculine in 'one' (*echad*), the same adjective used for the plural noun 'my God/Adonay' in the *Sh'ma* prayer; hence, the second line of the poem should literally be "peered from one faces." "Many waters" alludes to the *Song of Songs.*

TEFILLIN: *Tefillin*, usually translated "phylacteries," consist of two black leather boxes containing scriptural passages bound by black leather strips on the left hand and on the head, and worn for morning services on all days of the year except Sabbath and Holy Days.

In four passages in the Bible there occur almost identical phrases requiring the male Jew to put "thee words" (of the Law) for a "sign upon thy hand and a frontlet between thine eyes." In two of the passages it literally says "you shall bind them." There are strict rules governing the material of the boxes, the straps, and the parchment on which scripture and god's name is written, as well as the arrangement and tying of the straps and the order in which they are to be bound. The duty of wearing *tefillin* begins when a boy reaches thirteen. The wearing of *tefillin* induces a serious frame of mind. Hence, Wallach's poem "Tefillin" provoked and enraged many of her readers.

MAKE ME A DOUBLE: Wallach's references to her double, including pronouns, adjectives and verbs, are in the masculine form. I used 'he' rather than 'who' in the first verse in order to make that clear from the start.

LET THE WORDS: *min* (pronounced *meen*) means *sex* or *gender*, it also means *kind* or *type*. I translated the line *C'mo sh'ten min haim la'mila* "like giving a kind of life to the word" because of the construction *min haim*, a kind of life. (Sex-life would be *hayee min*.)

BOURGEOIS: in these lines Wallach is playing with the word *ha-makom*, "the place," and "The Place," which is one of God's names; she is also making use of the slang for *ba'makom*, or 'in the place,' meaning 'on the spot.'

HEBREW: "without cover of tongue," in Hebrew *bli ki-sut lashon*. In my earlier translation of this poem I translated the phrase 'with a free tongue' which eliminated the strangeness of the literal meaning but it also reduced Wallach's "without cover" to 'free,' leaving out the sexually interesting hide-and-seek activity of the tongue/language.

A MAN NOT MAN/A WOMAN NOT WOMAN: "faceless" in Hebrew *bli partzuf*; Wallach uses the word *panim* for the physical face (as well as the word *bfnim* from the same root to mean 'inside') everywhere else in the poem. *Partzuf* usually refers to the look on one's face, or facial expression, as in "to make a face."

MASTURBATION: mr. man not: *mar eesh lo* in lines 1 and 10 could be mr. no man except that Wallach reverses the order later in the poem in lines 17, 18, 43, 76, and 95 when it is clearly 'no man' *lo eesh* and 'mr. no man,' *mar lo eesh*. Very bitter: *mar kol kach* in line 6 could also be 'mr. so very so': *mar* in Hebrew means both mister and bitter. "With hands of air" is the literal translation for *bi-day avir*; *bi-day* "with hands of" is usually used to mean "through [the air]."

WERE YOU ABROAD: abroad: *b'hutz la'aretz*, literally "outside The Land", i.e. outside of Israel

MY SINS: "O bonny... O my builder:" *boni* could be either 'my builder' or 'bonny'; the poem is addressed to a masculine addressee, perhaps God, or as in the Robert Burns poem "O my bonny..."

UNFINISHED LOVE SONG: "during surgery:" *b'nituach* literally means 'during/in cutting, operation, or surgery'; it also means 'during analysis,' both psychological and literary/aesthetic.

IN A STRANGE NEST: Yona: a dove. It is also a male and female name, the poet's first name.

AND I BEING MYSELF: "Immortality of the soul:" *hisharut hanefesh*, literally, 'the remaining soul' or 'the soul that remains,' a phrase used in Jewish philosophy to describe life after death.

ABOUT THE AUTHOR

Yona Wallach was born in Tel Aviv, Israel in 1944, and died in 1985 of breast cancer. She was raised in the town of Kiryat Ono of which her father was a founder. He died in the War of Independence when she was a young child. From the start, with the publication of *Things* in 1966, she was hailed a poet of demonic power. As one of the groundbreaking "Tel Aviv Poets" circle which emerged around the journals *Achshav* and *Siman Kriah* in the 1960s, Wallach's work came to full force in the wake of the Yom Kippur War. She exemplifies those Hebrew writers who for the first time were shaping the language as native speakers. She dared to present herself as a blasphemous woman, shifting from childish innocence to blatant sexuality, as no woman writer in Hebrew had done before. She was a frequent contributor to Israeli literary periodicals, and won the Prime Minister's Literary Prize for her poetry in 1978. She also wrote for and appeared with Israeli rock groups. A record of her readings/musical performances was issued in 1982. She wrote throughout her life with a sense of freedom, unflagging inspiration, heightened consciousness, extraordinary energy. Her other books include *Two Gardens* (1969), *Collected Poems* (1976), *Wild Light* (1983), *Forms* (1985) and *Appearance* (1985). *Subconscious Opens Like a Fan: Selected Poems of Yona Wallach* was first published in Israel in 1992 and is now in its 12th printing.

ABOUT THE TRANSLATOR

Linda Stern Zisquit has published three collections of poetry, *Ritual Bath* (1993), *Unopened Letters* (1996) and *The Face in the Window* (2004). Her translations from Hebrew include *Desert Poems of Yehuda Amichai*, *The Book of Ruth,* and *Wild Light: Selected Poems of Yona Wallach* (Sheep Meadow Press, 1997) for which she received an NEA Translation Grant and was short-listed for a PEN Translation Award. She lives in Israel where she teaches at Bar Ilan University, and runs Artspace, a Jerusalem art gallery representing contemporary Israeli artists.